Discovering Music

Developing the Music Curriculum in Secondary Schools

Keith Swanwick
Dorothy Taylor

Batsford Academic and Educational Ltd
London

Typeset by Tek-Art Ltd, London SE20
and printed in Great Britain by
Billing & Son Ltd,
Worcester
for the publishers
Batsford Academic and Educational Ltd
an imprint of B T Batsford Ltd
4 Fitzhardinge Street
London W1H 0AH

British Library Cataloguing in Publication Data
Swanwick, Keith
    Discovering music.
    1. Music—Instruction and study
    I. Title   II. Taylor, Dorothy
    780'.7'2   MT1

ISBN 0 7134 4065 1

780.72
ℒ 972 d $K_{\bot}$

216464

Acknowledgment

We wish to thank those teachers whose work is a frequent
source of encouragement and has influenced the development
of ideas in this book. We also acknowledge the secretarial and
typing skills of Margaret Clements who cheerfully and effectively
sorted out our manuscripts into legible documents.

Contents

Foreword

The approach to the secondary and middle school curriculum outlined in this book is based on substantial teaching experience and involvement in teacher education. It is a new approach in the sense that curriculum suggestions usually either provide materials or confirm or challenge existing practice, while we are attempting to engender a *style* of curriculum development based on the simple principle of staying close to music. This, we hope, will help teachers to generate their own classroom strategies and assimilate these suggestions and others into sound and purposeful practice. What is not new, and can be found in the work and writing of all effective music educators, is the attempt to understand what is involved in music itself and what motivates human beings to learn.

Today it seems to matter more than in the past that we can be articulate about what we do in schools. We have to justify our decisions and negotiate our way in a world of shrinking funds and growing demands. Because of this we have given reasons behind our practical suggestions and have put forward a rationale within which specific curriculum activities can find a place. This is especially so in the first and last chapters and 'practical' people may be inclined to skip them. We would, however, urge readers to tackle these sections and, if necessary to read them more than once. They have been *written* more than once and we believe that they are important!

Keith Swanwick
Dorothy Taylor

1
Purpose in Music Education

One of the most urgent tasks for teachers of music, especially those teaching music in schools, is to find some kind of basis on which to build a worthwhile and purposeful musical curriculum. The lack of purpose that is so often evident communicates itself to pupils in school, especially those in secondary schools, and makes music appear to be an aimless and rather arbitrary subject which varies enormously from school to school and teacher to teacher. The rediscovery of purposefulness is therefore a prime need at this time. However, along with a sense of purpose must go the flexibility required for different groups of children, different types of school and widely differing teacher strengths and weaknesses.

MAKING A CURRICULUM
There are several different ways of setting about the task of making a music curriculum. The most common way, and the least structured, is for teachers to amplify their own enthusiasms, to notice which of these seem to be accepted by classes and to work on this. Unfortunately the result of this approach is a kind of 'rag-bag' of activities where any sense of purpose is very weak. There will inevitably be many flat spots during the time given over to music, if this curriculum model prevails, due to the arbitrary selection of activities.

A second way of constructing a music curriculum is to identify particular skills and concepts and to develop these through appropriate activities. Unfortunately, this often results in second-hand activities where music itself becomes subordinate to teaching something else. For example, we might find ourselves choosing particular tunes, not for their musical quality but because they illustrate some point of notation or because they are examples of a particular style or composer or because they develop certain rhythmic skills. The most highly organised and systematic of such courses would be something along the lines of the Kodaly system of carefully graded material. However, we ought to remember that Kodaly was a composer of considerable stature and it is not surprising that the Kodaly Choral Method contains a wealth of satisfying music, even though much of it was composed for didactic reasons.

The approach to curriculum building advocated in this book is one which stays very close to first-hand musical experience for the teacher and the pupils. We are taking as a basic assumption the view that music education is essentially about developing what might be called musical *appreciation*. By this we do not necessarily mean using records or tapes of music along with details and information about the composer or the work itself but rather the ability, and it *is* an ability, to perceive what is going on in music and to respond to it with enjoyment and possibly delight. Whatever our pupils do out of school and when leaving school, we would want them to respond to a wide range of music in a positive and lively way. They may or may not be actively concerned in the world of amateur music-making, or become composers or professional performers. They may find their way into types of music that may not have featured very large in the school curriculum but we would hope that the work in school has developed the sense of the value of music and some glimpse of its power to engage us, to speak to us, and at the highest level to move us profoundly.

If we can accept that the main objective of all music education is to enable people to appreciate music, that is to value music as a life-enhancing experience, then we have not only the best possible basis on which to build a curriculum but also the only really satisfactory justification for music education that exists. We all recognise that human needs are not fully met by the provision of physical and material well-being. People need to make sense of their lives, to find living a rich and worthwhile experience. Evidence for this can be seen in the pervasive myths, rituals, ceremonies and artistic activities that are powerfully present in all cultures, whether in the East, in the Third World or in the Western tradition. Music, along with the other arts, satisfies a basic human need to make sense of life and to engage in rich experiences. Music is not an alternative to living but an enhancement of life. The role of a music teacher is therefore to develop the ability to respond to music in the fullest possible way across the widest range of experiences. Only the exceptionally gifted teacher can manage this intuitively and without prior thought, and it is impossible to conceive of any other profession that relies entirely on such exceptional gifts. However, most of us are 'good enough' teachers if we think out clearly what we are about and test what actually happens against some form of yardstick, noticing when we succeed and, perhaps more important, when we fail. Only in this way can we be said to be truly professional. In a quite frightening way teachers stand between pupils and music, sometimes acting as a window or an open door but at other times functioning only as an impediment, blocking off access to music itself. We can no longer afford to be amateurish.

MUSIC AND KNOWING

It may be that much of our difficulty comes from not recognising the different kinds of knowledge that are involved in musical experience. This is not as complicated or academic as it may sound. For example, it is very necessary at times for us to *know how* to do things, to operate a lathe, to spell a word, to translate a passage, to put our thoughts into a structured form, to manipulate a musical instrument, to use musical notation. Knowing how to do things is essentially the use and development of particular skills. The second most commonly understood kind of knowledge is *knowing that*. For example we may know that 2 + 7 makes 9 or that Manchester is 200 miles from London or that 'avoir' is the verb 'to have', or that Beethoven wrote nine symphonies, or what a note-row is. A further way of knowing is sometimes called knowledge by acquaintance, or in other words *knowing him, her or it*. For example, we may know Renoir's painting *The Rower's Lunch*, or know a friend or pupil, or know a city. This is the most important kind of knowing for music teachers. In music it is the specific knowledge of a particular musical work, the one we are listening to or the one we are composing or performing. For example, we might know *how* to manipulate technically a musical instrument and we might know *that* the piece we are playing is by Bartok but we would also need to know the piece *itself* and become aware of its particular character — its expressive quality and its structure — the way in which one part relates to another. The fourth way of knowing we might call knowing *what's what*, knowing what we really like, what matters to us; in other words — what we value. In case this seems somewhat theoretical let us consider a practical example. A child learning to play on the piano an easy piece by Bach, may be able to cope with the skills involved in playing the right notes at the right time. In other words she will know *how*. But she may also know *that* it is by Bach and may have some idea of what it is to play Bach in an appropriate style. However these kinds of knowing are by themselves insufficient. The pupil will also have to know *it*, the piece itself, the way in which the phrases are shaped, the way in which each note relates to each other note, the form determined by the cadences and something of the expressive potential of the piece which might be achieved by a choice of a particular speed and levels of loudness at different times. However, even if she knows how, knows that, and knows it she may well say 'But I don't like it'. In other words, the piece does not count as a valued experience. It does not fit in to the pupil's idea of *what's what*, but at least she will have reached a point where she can choose on a basis of experience.

The same kind of analysis can be applied to any musical activity in classrooms. For example, a class may play a twelve-bar blues improvisation at a fairly low level of skill (with very little know-how) but communicate the expressive qualities of the piece (knowing it). At the same time they may have more or less information about this particular musical form (knowing that) and may vary from individual to individual as to whether they find it of value or not (knowing what's what). Or again, when a small group is composing using a note-row the members might be very skilful in handling the instruments and the row, achieve a good sense of structure in the composition, be well-informed about serial techniques but find the activity boring — that is to say of little value for them. 'Knowing' is quite complicated and it is difficult for us to understand what is involved at times. It may be helpful therefore to keep these four rather crude categories in mind and we shall return to them later on. There is obviously a good deal of linking between them and for most pupils it will probably be true to say that if they achieve some skills, along with relevant information, while getting to grips with actual music (knowing it), then there will be a strong tendency to enjoy and value the activity. After all, we all tend to 'like what we know' as well as 'know what we like'.

Merely knowing how to do things or knowing something about music is no substitute for knowing music itself and finding enjoyment in the experience. Yet a tremendous proportion of teaching in music is devoted to knowing how or knowing that, while very little attention is given to knowing it, the music itself, partly because it is very difficult to find an appropriate language in which to discuss what happens in music itself. It is certainly not possible to come to the fourth way of knowing (knowing what's what) through direct teaching or persuasion. The way in which we value things has a great deal to do with our own personal development as human beings, our age, our social attitudes, the type of personality we are and the previous experiences we have undergone along with all the associations with music that have been built up. We can however do a great deal more than we often manage to achieve in the development of a vocabulary, a workshop language that enables us, where necessary, to talk with one another about music itself. Knowing *it* is our real goal and our language must serve this aim.

THE ELEMENTS OF MUSIC

Basically, as we hinted earlier, there are two elements to be taken into account. All music has *expressive character* or quality. That is to say, it is more or less active or fluid or angular or stationary, more or less dense or heavy, driving forward or holding back. Music can be spiky or flowing, smooth or cutting, expanding or contracting. Most of these and other expressive elements will not be revealed in traditional or any other form of notation. They are brought out by the manner of performance or develop in the aural imagination of the composer. Some conductors have the gift of communicating through gesture, the kind of weight and size, the ebb and flow of the music that makes it meaningful, that gives it expressive character. The second element is the *perceptible structure* of the music that is being experienced as composer, performer or listener; fundamentally the relationship between different materials and ideas. This involves the awareness of the significance of change, recognition of the scale on which events take place, a sense of what is normal in a particular context and what is surprising or strikingly different. We shall call the perception of these elements *musical understanding*. Because this is such an important concept we must consider it further at this point.

MUSICAL UNDERSTANDING

Musical understanding obviously depends to some extent, on various kinds of skill and information, but it goes beyond these and is able to be described in terms of structure and expressive character in the following way:

1 *Structure*: the relationships of part to part and part to

whole. Structural understanding implies more than labelling musical forms such as Ternary or Rondo. It involves perceiving the way in which one idea follows another and what the effect of repetition is or how strongly contrasted parts of the music are. There can be no musical understanding away from *particular* pieces of music, whether we compose, perform or listen to them.

Repetition and contrast are the main features of musical structure and the most easily understood. All other structural devices are derived from these. The following are examples of this:

Repetition	*Contrast*
ostinato	change of figure
motif	extension, fragmentation
theme	middle section, episode
tonic key	transposition, modulation, chromaticism
beat	off-beat, syncopation
'air'	variation
recapitulation	development
fugue subject	augmentation, diminution
note-row	inversion, retrograde motion
'natural' sound	electronic distortion

These kinds of repetition and contrast can be identified in conventional musical forms such as binary structures in simple songs; binary short movements in Bach, Handel, Purcell; extended binary movements as in Scarlatti piano Sonatas; the extension of binary to simple sonata form, as in the first movement of Mozart's *Eine Kleine Nacht-musik*, or in simple variation form, rondo, fugue, or the contrasts and similarities of pitch, timbre and levels of loudness in a work such as Berio's *Sequenza V*.

2 *Expressive character*: mood, atmosphere, changing levels of tension and resolution, display of feeling or emotion, impression, dramatic and operatic devices. Expressive character is most obvious in opera, oratorio and programme music and in the works of 'Romantic' composers where there is some connection with nature, the composer's life, literature or stories. However, even the 'purest' music, such as a Bach Fugue or Invention has a clear character that can be grasped or missed by the performer or listener. It may be bold, lilting, resolute, flowing, march-like, lively, solemn, etc. The expressive character of music can be explored in many simple ways, for example, by varying the speed and loudness of a well-known song or by composing a short piece (perhaps in a group) using only three

notes but controlling the speed and loudness and texture (two or more notes at once) to achieve a building up of tension.

Expressive character is determined by such things as pitch register, pitch intervals, phrase shapes, *tempi*, rate of acceleration or retardation, degree of smoothness or detachedness, accentuation, metre, density of texture. It is important that children explore these things for themselves, making choices in performance and composition, as well as identifying them in other people's music. When recorded music is used it is best to find pieces that are strongly characterised, especially for younger children, not too long and with some changes of character that can be identified and discussed. Several listenings will be required to attain the necessary familiarity to identify the more subtle aspects of the particular character of any piece of music. The range of styles ought to be as wide as possible including the traditional works but including also different kinds of ethnic, folk and pop music, and the music of contemporary composers. It is better to discuss rather than tell classes what to expect. We can ask 'What is it like?' and 'How is it done?' For this reason heavily pre-scripted works, such as *Peter and the Wolf*, have less educational value.

Bearing in mind that what we have called Musical Understanding is central to music education, it becomes obvious that this understanding can only result from direct contact with music as *composer*, *performer* and *listener*. Alternative activities, such as copying down notes on the lives of great composers, or answering questions on instruments of the orchestra, or undertaking a project from resource books on acoustics or opera should always be related to direct musical experience in one of the three central activities.

When we perform, compose or listen to music we are not of course necessarily conscious of expressive character and structure as separate entities. However, because teachers stand between music and other people, and because it is essential to develop helpful ways of talking about music with one another, we shall find it useful to bear in mind expressive character and structure as two sides of a single coin. Our own critical faculties will be sharpened, and, in the best sense of the word, a teacher will often be functioning as a kind of *critic*, acutely perceiving what is happening and responding to it in an appropriate way. We should at least be able to ask good questions. What would it be like if you left out this section or made it longer? What would happen if we took more time over making this crescendo?

What difference does it make if the lower instruments play louder and the higher ones quieter?

We can see what happens if we take as a simple example the well known Jewish round *Shalom Chaverin*

WHAT WOULD HAPPEN IF?

What would happen if we sang this tune as a brisk march? What would it be like if we sang it with a heavy accent on the first beat of the bar as though it were a work song or a stomping dance? How would it be if we sang it very quietly, smoothly and slowly, as though it were a distant memory gently coming back to us? If we were teaching this song to a class we might well want to raise these kinds of questions and find words like 'heavy' or 'driving' or 'holding back' or 'gentle' to describe the expressive character of particular performances. We might also want to explore the structural elements by having the second alternate phrases sung by different sections of the class to point up the answering function of these phrases, or to compare the 'unfinished' quality of the second phrase with the stronger finality of the last. The fusion of expressive and structural elements is felt in the movement out and up towards the middle of the tune and the retracting, returning movement to the end. The sense of arrival and finality can be enhanced by repeating the figure several times, the sound gradually dying away.

So much is now open to us. The class might get into small groups and choose their own way of performing the song, bringing out its expressive possibilities — like a march, a dance, a lament, flowing, spiky, heavy, light. Or they might compose a free texture of sound that has the same kind of structure — statement followed by response. Or using a few notes of a mode or scale they might compose and perform their own tune with a 'going away' and 'coming back' to the home-note. Or the words can be taken and used as sound materials for a voice composition: each of the nine syllables has its own special sound and fascinating pieces can be composed using just three or four of these.

The richness of possibilities stems from knowing *it*, the round itself. Knowing *how* has played its role incidentally; knowing how to pronounce the words, how to sing in tune and in time. Knowing *that* may also take its place; knowing that the song has a Jewish context, that it is in $\frac{3}{4}$ time, that it is in the Aeolian mode, though all this seems less essential than knowing how. Ultimately though, both these ways of knowing stop short of the experience and possibilities of this song, this particular 'it'. Only when we begin to think about its expressive and structural elements does a world of implications open up for us. Instead of being driven into dead-ends of skills and information *for their own sake*, the road ahead becomes open with a multitude of alternative ways leading off in various directions. Teachers and pupils are all learners, exploring the possibilities generated by an encounter with a particular tune.

DISCOVERY

What we are advocating then is that all encounters with music ought to have about them an element of *discovery*. The problem is that for many of us elements of discovery and the excitement of discovering are buried beneath knowledge that has been acquired in other ways and at other times. Many children, let alone teachers, are ready to give up the effort of discovering and put in its place an acceptance of received information. We all too easily sell our birthright of natural curiosity in exchange for the comforting certainties of the familiar. Effective teaching depends in part upon the recognition of this and requires us to structure carefully what we do, to maximize the potential for truly musical encounters in the classroom. The succeeding chapters in this book give some ideas for developing this approach in a purposeful rather than an aimless and careless way.

One of the bonuses of adopting the notion of discovery as central to music teaching, is that it cuts across all kinds of arguments and problems that have perplexed people for many years. Discovery can happen whether we are composers, performers or in audience. Discovery can happen whether the music we are handling belongs to the classical tradition, the East, jazz, pop, rock, reggae or the many shades of contemporary music. We can rediscover something we thought we already knew or open up a totally unexplored territory. To get on the inside of this experience it is important for teachers too to feel a sense of curiosity and discovery frequently and powerfully. Too often we are content with the second-hand and the second-rate. We use course-books or other peoples' ideas mechanically and sometimes blindly. We set our pupils tasks that are unmusical, unexciting. We become dulled and stale by repetition. The procedures we are suggesting here may help to rejuvenate teaching and to give it direction, purpose and imaginative quality.

Because teaching is demanding and complex we need a fundamental, simple and powerful set of working principles. The first of these stems from the discussion so far. We must be true to music, that is to say we must provide our pupils with experience of the stuff itself, knowledge of *it*, the integrity of the particular. The second principle has to do with what motivates pupils as people, with the mainsprings of human behaviour, the dynamic forces that propel us all.

MOTIVATION

Basically and naturally and in the beginning everyone wants to learn, to achieve mastery, to develop. Unfortunately this natural impulse is often stunted by pressures exerted by teachers and schools. Children are put through an incredible series of 'educational' hoops: heavy timetables, rigorous social and academic demands, days spent switching from the thought processes of one subject to another and yet again another. We impose a whole range of extrinsic reasons for learning, that is to say not to do with the quality of the experience itself but with success in tests, examinations, in the achievement of good reports and so on. Yet surely we ought to be searching for the deep wells of human motivation that spring out of the qualities of the activities themselves. The stick and the carrot may be necessary at times but they should never be regarded as fundamental. We can gain insights here from the thinking of one of our most influential psychologists, Jerome Bruner.

'The will to learn is an intrinsic motive, one that finds both its source and its reward in its own exercise. The will to learn becomes a 'problem' only under specialized circumstances like those of a school, where a curriculum is set, students confined and the path fixed. The problem exists not so much in learning itself, but in the fact that what the school imposes often fails to enlist the natural energies that sustain spontaneous learning — curiosity, a desire for competence, aspiration to emulate a model, and a deep-sensed commitment to the web of social reciprocity.'   (Towards a Theory of Instruction, page 127)

This passage has about it a certain 'ring of truth' and we would do well to consider the implications for teaching and learning in music.

If we are to tap those natural sources of energy then every learner has to become *involved* and active. So much music teaching seems concerned with handing out information. How often do we ask children what they notice in music rather than tell them what they should 'know' about it? How frequently is there note-taking rather than discussion — a dialogue of discovery? Music is especially unsuited to this approach. Coming to musical perceptions, making choices and decisions in composition and performance, recognising the preferences of oneself and other people; these are much more central to musical experience than providing 'correct' answers. How are we to engage in music education unless we provide frequent opportunities for the development of these elements? Long ago the Greek philosopher Socrates saw this clearly. The ultimate and ever-present objective in teaching is to guide the learner to the point where he sees things for himself, one could say, to a point where teachers become redundant. This affirms that learning in music ought to be a succession of discoveries linked with a feeling of personal mastery, thus drawing on what Bruner calls curiosity and a desire for competence. Because these discoveries take place alongside other people, especially in the peer group of a school class, the 'commitment to social reciprocity' of which Bruner speaks is also engaged. There is a substantial difference between the competition of tests, examinations and reports, and the stimulation of the achievements of others along with the sympathy engendered by any difficulties experienced by them.

The 'aspiration to emulate a model' is also part of the fabric of peer-group interaction. There are important implications here for the development of small group work.

The teacher him or herself of course is a crucial model and this demands that whatever is done should be done, as far as possible, in a way that is true to music, totally musical. The teacher is much more than a benevolent ring-master as he directs, guides and shares discovery with his pupils. In demonstrating his *own* curiosity, desire for competence, admiration for good models, and commitment to the group, a powerful motivating force is released.

A MODEL OF MUSICAL KNOWING

Finally, we need to clarify ways in which pupils become active in music and the roles they play. These have been discussed in *A Basis for Music Education* (Keith Swanwick 1979) but it may be helpful now to remind ourselves of the model suggested in that book. There are five parameters of musical experience — three of them directly relating to music and two more having supporting and enabling roles, easily remembered by the device C(L)A(S)P.

C	Composition	formulating a musical idea, making a musical object
(L)	Literature studies	the literature of and the literature about music ·
A	Audition	responsive listening as (though not necessarily in) an audience
(S)	Skill acquisition	aural, instrumental, notational
P	Performance	communicating music as a 'presence'

This way of identifying the activities relating to music has proved helpful in many ways. For example, it reminds us of the centrality of *Audition*, that particular kind of listening when we are really *understanding* music and not just spotting tunes, or dominant sevenths or identifying composer or performer. It also picks out the three clusters of activity when we directly relate to music; composition, audition and performance. Observations made in large numbers of classrooms suggest that teachers spend most time trying to improve skills or adding to knowledge of literature studies, more time than they in fact predict or estimate. Some teachers have found it helpful to prepare for or to analyse their teaching along the lines of these five parameters, bearing in mind that we often move very quickly from one to another and that one kind of activity relates to the others.

There can however be some confusion between an activity, what is *done* and what is acquired *through* the activity, what is *learned*. For example someone might be playing tennis, that would be the activity, but she may, as a result of playing tennis, improve her service or come to watch the ball better or even come to realise what a difficult game it is to play well! These things would be what is *learned* and such changes in levels of skill and attitude would still persist when the particular game was over. The improved service would still exist in a future game (provided it was not too far in the future!) and the learned attitude about the difficulty of the game could be a topic of conversation when not playing and would certainly influence the play on subsequent occasions. The instance of tennis is particularly apt. A recent report on tennis in Britain concludes that too much emphasis has been placed on isolated skills, such as serving or using a backhand and not enough emphasis has been placed on a *feeling* for the game, developing a sense of competition, determination, flexibility and total involvement. In other words, isolated skill practice may not bring about *understanding* of what tennis is really about. We might find parallels in music, an emphasis on skills (scales) or on factual knowledge of one kind or another in the area of Literature Studies.

We have tried to indicate earlier in this chapter what we mean by *musical understanding*. This must surely be at the heart of our teaching though we would still look for certain learning of skills and information (from now we shall call the area of Literature Studies *information*). Once we have identified particular areas in which we expect or hope that learning will take place we can then begin to be more precise about our objectives as teachers. The sharpest and clearest way of formulating objectives is to preface every statement we make about our music curriculum with the phrase 'the pupils should be able to . . .'. These will be the learning outcomes of the particular activities and it is vital that we realise that activities themselves may not bring about learning, a fact that sometimes escapes us and gives rise to classroom practice that could hardly be said to be education in any real sense of the term.

In the final chapter we shall turn to this again. In the meantime we need only to register that doing things is not the same as learning things. The following illustration may make this clear. The three columns in the following diagram represent the three areas where we can formulate teaching and learning objectives. They are, *Understanding*, *Skills* and *Information*. Information relates, of course, to what we have previously called Literature Studies. The activities we have in mind are mainly in the areas of Composition, Performance and Audition (active listening) relating to the round *Shalom Chaverin* which we examined earlier in this chapter.

Objectives: the pupils should be able to:

Understanding	Skills	Information
Perform in class and smaller groups with the character of a march, a work-song, a lament;	Sing back each phrase accurately; sing the whole tune from memory;	
Choose *one* instrument to enhance the effect; identify phrases that 'reach out' and those that 'draw back'.	Recognise differences of loud/soft and smooth/detached; beat in $\frac{2}{4}$ time to the music at different speeds	Say what *Shalom Chaverin* means and what language it is. Explain and demonstrate what an accent is.
In small groups compose and perform a short piece using the sounds 'Sha', 'Lom', 'Averin', choosing the order, the speed and levels of loudness to make an interesting and expressive composition.	Demonstrate ensemble skills, starting together, listening to each other.	
Suggest titles that describe the compositions of other groups.		

These are not just 'activities' but are demonstrations of abilities which are 'taken away' and can be extended in the future.

To summarise, we are advocating an approach to music education which emphasises the following:

1   Delight in music, a rich appreciation is our aim.

2   Discovery is central to musical activities and the crucial
     questions are: What is it (like)? and What happens if . . . .?
3   Through the activities of composition, performance and
     listening we shall be looking for the development of skills,
     information, musical understanding and valuing, with
     understanding as central.
4   Teaching and learning should be so organised as to draw on
     the natural energies of motivation common to everyone.

The ideas and suggestions presented in the following chapters
should be regarded only as examples and must be approached
in a sufficiently flexible way so as to meet the individual
settings of teachers in terms of resources, personal strengths and
particular pupils. This book is not a course to be followed but a
guide to curriculum development in music, showing how worthwhile and musical activities can be generated and sustained in
the classroom. Many of the illustrations are drawn from classroom practice and a number of the musical examples are fairly
commonplace, deliberately so.

Each teacher will need to explore for him or herself what is
possible but this does not mean that anything goes. We shall
have before us two challenging questions which must be asked
about any classroom activity. Is it musical? This implies that
we are beyond mere skills and information and that what we
have called 'musical understanding' is taking place. Is there a
sense of achievement? This involves a sense of going beyond
where we were before and discovering music for ourselves as
should the pupils for themselves. We may not always succeed in
this but if we are not prepared to try there seems little point in
bothering with music in school at all.

In the next chapter, with the aid of some easily accessible
examples, we shall try to tease out for ourselves what is involved in musical understanding. We shall concentrate especially
on *expressive character*, since this is often found to be a difficult idea. Our aim here is to explore some music for ourselves.
The subsequent chapters will then deal with classroom possibilities.

2
Starting with Music

To illustrate the approach described in the opening chapter let us examine three pieces of music, contrasting in style and in medium. The first is for keyboard, the second a song with piano accompaniment and the third for wind ensemble. However familiar these examples may be, we are attempting to listen with fresh ears, with, as it were, some naiveté.

Example 1   *Polonaise in G minor*, No. 12, from *A Little Note-Book for Anna Magdalena Bach* by J S Bach

First we ought to play through this short piece to feel its totality before going back to the beginning. Let us play the first two bars again.

What is most striking about this opening statement? Is the music *placid* or is it *energetic*? Is it *gentle* or somewhat *aggressive*?

Although we shall inevitably be individual in our choice of language when describing music, it is obvious that the adjectives 'placid' and 'gentle' would be completely inappropriate. On the other hand the terms 'energetic' and 'aggressive' would clearly come close to describing the expressive quality of the music; that is to say as close as any verbal language can come to describing the subtleties of musical expression.

At this point we can ask ourselves which musical elements give, or contribute to, this energetic, vigorous characteristic. For example:

— Is it in part due to the fact that the musical idea or statement is a single strand, reinforced at the octave?
— Could it result from the characteristic ♫ rhythmic unit?
— from the affirmative ♩ on the third beat . . . or the leap down to the accented crochet?

We might ask . . . is it the uncertainty of ending the first bar on E♭ and the second bar on D? If we try other alternatives for these accented notes how effective are they? Are some more effective than others? Does the mood change — a little, a lot, not substantially? Does the editor's 'forte' marking substantially contribute to the expressive quality?

If we now proceed to the next two bars we ask ourselves the same questions: is the music *placid* or *energetic*, *gentle* or *aggressive*?

. . . We might try to be more precise by searching for the adjective which most aptly describes the expressive quality of these two bars. At least we can list those terms which would *not* be appropriate eg 'spiky', 'energetic', 'aggressive', 'rough', and others that would such as 'smooth', 'regal', 'stately', 'secure', 'calm'.

We hear how the quality of the ♫ rhythm changes when, in its reversed form it becomes ♫ and how the fifth drop and sixth upward leap

have the effect of subtlely softening this same ♫ figure. This softer, smoother effect may also be helped by the steadier bass line and the descending thirds.

On to bars 9 to 12.

Although there is here a return to the opening ♫ figure, what aspect of this phrase gives the feeling that it should be played softly?

Might it be caused by the key change to B♭ major? or does it stem from the *upward* leap to the crotchet, or again is it due to the editor's 'piano' markings?

Moving on, the ♫ figure is presented in new guise as it oscillates around the C and E♭ inverted pedal point:

bars 13 and 14.

Again we may ask the same questions in deciding what, essentially, is the expressive quality of the music and how has this been achieved. Is the upper part's *tranquillity* and *steadiness* achieved because of the pedal point, or the consonant thirds? Is this quality reinforced by the strong and mobile bass?

Again in bars 17 to 20

the listener hears another change of quality . . . to *gracefulness*, *finesse*, *delicacy*, *lightness*?

Why? If we look at the upper part, the arpeggiated figure suggests an upward light and floating movement,

and in the bass that same figure appears to take on a more aggressive role as a result of holding the quaver over the bar-line, eg

By asking ourselves such questions, by acute aural observation we have begun to reach the inside of Bach's Polonaise. Furthermore, we have begun to make a form of deep analysis through concentrating on the music's *expressive* qualities. In turn we may help our pupils to become involved with this (and all kinds of) music by penetrating music's "meaning"; by involving them actively in handling musical elements before going on to the supportive facts and information about the piece itself.

At this point it may be relevant to ask: 'What is a Polonaise?' The accentuation of the third beat has already been perceived and experienced and is now more meaningful to any discussion which may arise about the dance form, its origin, its history, etc. Similarly if the composition is in any way *valued*, information will be easily found from written sources about the composer, his times, keyboard instruments of the day, and so on.

From this specific example, individual teachers will see the possibilities of applying the model in working with different age groups. If the example were taken further with advanced students the following avenues might be explored:

— how many different rhythmic figures are there in this piece?
— examine the rhythmic intricacies — how does Bach delay accents, for example?
— work out the key structure; the architectural structure;
— pick out cadences or points of repose;
— what is the implied harmony of the crotchets in bars 1 and 2, try alternatives and then eliminate;
— examine the texture (2 parts, 3 parts; does it ever have more?);
— experiment with timbre (arrange for wind, strings, voice; eg in the style of the Swingle Singers).

This list does not exhaust the possibilities by any means, but gives some indications for further exploration and discovery.

Example 2   *The Birds Lament* from *The Aviary* by Richard Rodney Bennett for unison voices and piano

In this example we benefit from the fact that the composer is still alive. We can be assured that the tempo and dynamic markings are his. Here there is the extra dimension of contrasting vocal with keyboard sound and the expressive quality of language itself to be taken into account.

In essence this song evokes the individual characteristics of five birds, the linnet, jay, rook, crow and thrush, as they nostalgically sing of their partners, who have forsaken them.

First we might perform the song at a pace which appears both appropriate to a 'lament' and comfortable to the singer. In fact a certain degree of experimentation with tempi would be appropriate here. Then we could check the metronomic marking given at the start, ie *con moto ♩*=126 and compare a performance at this speed with our own interpretation of the tempo. The significant question is, therefore, does a 'lament' need to be slow in order to convey a quality of sadness, or 'lamenting'?

If we agree that the composer has achieved a quality of nostalgic sadness which comes across irrespective of the tempo chosen let us look in detail at the musical elements which may contribute to this quality.

First here are four bars of introduction:

Does this feel like one phrase, or two? Notice the unequivocal diatonicism of the first and third bars contrasting with the coloured uncertainty of the second and third. There is movement in the arpeggiated figure, taking off as if in flight, conveying perhaps a feeling of optimism before coming to land on the chords in bars two and four. There is doubt and uncertainty here, as the falling figure in the treble suggests:

and is reinforced by the colour of the chords themselves. If we experiment with the first chord making it a simple B minor root position or seventh chord we hear how fundamental the G natural is to the sad quality and the feeling of this bar. Furthermore, it is the juxtaposition, of this G natural against A, (this major second conflict as it were) which determines the quality of this first phrase and sets the tonal context for the song itself:

In bar 4, again the arpeggiated figure comes to rest, this time on yet a more enigmatic chromatic chord. Again there is the major second in the middle of the harmony (E and F#). How easy it would have been to have written this:

but how beautifully subtle and inspiring to hear this instead:

And so we begin verse one:

The vocal line, like the piano introduction, has an upward soaring quality before it swoops down on the words 'sing' and later on 'spring'. Is this feeling of upward movement heightened by the bass part which moves calmly in the opposite direction?

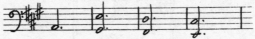

We hear the plain A major chord move into a succession of 7th and 9th chords, with again this haunting 2nd conflict characterising the inner moving part. The vocal line undulates upwards and downwards . . . 'And ne-ver-more will I be seen' . . .

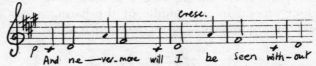

Notice how the melancholic feeling increases from this point onwards with a telling G ninth, E minor seventh

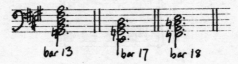

and F seventh harmonic structure before working back to A major and into the second verse which is a repeat of the first.

The second time bars or interlude move the song towards an abrupt change of mood in the third verse. Rooks and crows, their blackness, size and perhaps aggression, are conveyed through music which is significantly angular. The tonality sounds heavy and dark (C minor), the vocal line leaps and plummets and there are interesting heavy accentuations as both melody and support are suspended over from bar to bar:

If we repeat over and over the words 'rook', 'crow' there is a sound quality about the words themselves which contrasts strongly with the delicacy and lightness of the 'linnet' in verse one. Note however, that even in the midst of all this 'Sturm und Drang' there is a lightness of quality in the phrase 'Because our love . . . . '

Does this work so well because the right hand piano part is an octave higher than the voice? Yet the shrieks which follow are loud and piercing. The right hand piano accompaniment is still an octave higher, yet these shrieks appear far more dramatic than would be the case if the piano part followed the vocal line exactly.

The verse subsides to a gentle close before the piano returns with an emphatic dominant (but note the crunching second):

to A major for the last verse; a repeat of the music to verses one and two.

This song is rich in expressive quality and many of these musical elements might be taken as a basis for classwork. 'Seconds', for example, could form the basis for group composition or the differing effects of major and minor seconds explored. A simple chord progression might be used as a basis for experimenting with accompaniments and layouts, stimulated by the figurations in this song. 'Flight' could be used as the theme for a composition expressing the same qualities of lightness evoked by *The Birds Lament* eg 'upward soaring', 'plummeting', 'gliding'. Similarly, composition could be based on exploring mood contrasts such as 'light-sad', 'light-cheerful', 'heavy-sad', 'heavy-cheerful', etc. And, of course, a search could be made for comparisons in other works featuring birds (Respighi's *The Birds* — Prelude, Dove, Hen, Nightingale and Cuckoo; Beethoven's *Pastoral Symphony*, Sant Saens' *Carnival of the Animals* and Haydn's *Bird Quartet*). By comparison we do not mean the use of music to define or illustrate stereotyped images of birds or birdsong. Instead, when referring to other musical examples, it is the particularity of the piece which is important, as is the necessary teaching strategy which will lead pupils to make informed and perceptive judgements.

Example 3   *Serenade for Ten Wind Instruments*, Opus 44 by Dvořák, First Movement

If one had access to a score of this work, how tempting it would be to go immediately to the score and follow it while listening to the music. However, in line with our approach which advocates acute aural observation, let us build up our own basic working score from scratch. Little by little, with frequent playing and replaying, we will be able to exercise our aural skills and perceptions and to delve deeply into the music. This should provide us with a greater chance of taking it into our own experience. In other words, we shall be in a much better position to really know 'it', the music itself.

The first and over-riding impression which we have after listening to the opening eight bars is of a 'stately', 'processional' piece. There is a feeling of precision, one might say of 'measured tread' set from the first two beats of the opening phrase:

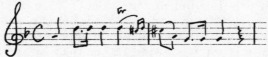

What is it about the music which gives it this characteristic quality? We may notice that there is a full wind sonority, a dense chordal texture as, for the most part, the parts move rhythmically together. Clearly the tempo is that of a moderate, measured walk. We may perceive that it is in quadruple time and in a minor key. There is also a prevalent dotted rhythm ♩♪ on a repeated note: eg

and a singularly interesting ornamentation (turn) which tends to occur in the first bar of each phrase of the first section or section A. We notice too, in the fourth bar, the reinforcement or extension of the cadence by the ♫ figure;

If we were to examine each of these factors in isolation, some might evoke this composite 'stately' or 'regal' quality more readily than others. Taken in combination however, as they are in this particular piece of music, we are left in no doubt of the overall processional movement as the essential quality of the opening section.

What else do we hear in the first eight bars?
There is the 'lift', a more expansive quality which affects the sixth bar with the C major chord and subsequent modulation to F major. Texturally there is the movement in the bass

whenever the melodic line is static. Notice how these eight bars are immediately repeated yet how differently they sound. Although melodically and harmonically there appears to be no change, in texture the whole effect is lighter or less dense. The musical effect is of a much gentler character. How has this been achieved?

First we may notice that the oboes this time feature prominently on the melodic line, or is it that fewer instruments are playing? Which instruments are silent? Like the oboe, the bassoon is now more in evidence as it is heard playing a bouncy Alberti-like bass(♫♫ ♫♫)and it would appear that in this repeat the emphasis is on woodwind rather than brass instrumental colour.

As we move on to bars 17 to 20 there is a brief passage featuring first the oboe and then the clarinet in interplay with reiterated chords on the horns; a kind of linking passage before the opening statement makes its return. It is interesting to note that, although Dvořák utilises the same ♩♫ rhythmic figure, the effect of the rising 'soh-ray' (A to E) interval appears less assertive and more questioning than 'soh-doh' (A to D). Is this heightened by the ornamentation (the trill and the semi-quaver)?

The section comes to a close with a repeat of the first eight bars. What happens next?

Immediately there is a communicated feeling of flow, of smoothness and lightness. Why? We hear that the music moves easily downwards by step. We also realise that the texture is more dispersed with woodwind solos on clarinet and oboe, in a form of dialogue.

Melodically the line is composed of short, descending phrases.

Rhythmically, the composer uses the same organic ♫ figure yet the musical quality expressed is quite different from that of the opening statement where the ♫ dotted rhythm repeats the same note and is less *legato*.

The feeling of lightness is further increased, one could say to one of delicacy, as the descending melodic fragments are repeated with decorative semiquavers played quietly

and then the semiquaver figure is taken up and elaborated by the oboe as the cadence is extended and reinforced:

We find that, in fact, this semiquaver figure is used and developed extensively over the next passage as a feeling of expectancy is gradually built up before the inevitable return of the opening statement.

Interesting in the extensive bridging section is the וּנָטַ phrase ending. The significant difference between this and the phrase ending of the opening four bars is the second beat ♩. The וְנָטַ element takes over the predominant role. Melodically the repeated rising intervals, thrown back and forth between woodwind, brass and bass strings:

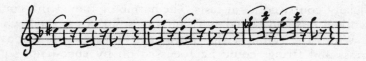

are treated in such a way that the return of section A appears even more majestic than before.

This time there is some development as the modulatory figure is not allowed to move into F major as it did before, but to G minor and back to D:

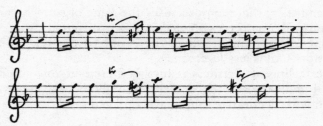

There is a brief reminder of:

this time in the home key and echoed by the cellos and bas-
soons and a feeling of gradual unwinding as the whole movement slows down with the following figure alternating in strings
and horns:

before the closing chords.

By now, with repeated hearings, we find ourselves with not
only a basic skeletal score of this particular movement but also
a more acute, deep knowledge of its structural elements and
expressive qualities. We could pursue the score — building
ideas still further to discover just how far our ears might take
us, adding the 'cello parts, for example, as they feature in the
alternate bars of the opening theme, or the echoing phrases in
the horns of the F major middle section. 'A' level pupils might
be encouraged to work in a similar fashion, enjoying the challenge of aural work based on 'real' music in contrast to arti-
ficially contrived aural tests. The harmonic framework could be
worked out and tested by comparing solutions at the keyboard.

With 16+ groups the distinctive timbres of woodwind,
brass and strings could be focussed on by encouraging pupils
to listen discriminatively in an informal quiz atmosphere. For
example, we might ask them to 'write down how many times
we hear the clarinet solo, or bass strings interjection' or
'is it strings alone?' or 'is it strings and bassoon?'. Let us refrain
from revealing the answer until attempts have been made to
discover the truth with our ears, before our eyes have sought

the sanctuary of the score with its conclusive visual proof.

One could use the basic score with both groups to show how organic this movement is, composed as it is with extreme economy from a basic two bar phrase (♪♫♪♬♪♫♫♪♪) . Pupils could be encouraged to use this movement as a model for their own compositions isolating the features of modulation, extension of cadence, climax building bridge passages, major endings to minor pieces or gently unwinding closing sections.

In the general music class, group composition could be encouraged in very specific ways eg 'Work out a short piece of music which could be used for a procession'. Alternatively: 'devise a piece in A B form with plenty of repeated notes in one section and lots of stepwise movement in the other'. Other suggestions might include focussing on steady accelerations and decelerations, or a piece alternating ♫ dotted rhythms with ♫ smooth running duplets, or one contrasting minor thirds with major thirds.

This piece would appear to lend itself to interpretation in movement (an activity dealt with in more detail in the next chapter).

With its characteristic sectional contrasts, interplay of instrumental colour, changes of tempi, texture, dynamics and register, many ways might be found to interpret the music in movement and dance. Not least, exploration could be made to show in movement the proportional contrasts and degrees of 'strong/light', 'large/small', 'wide/narrow', 'high/low' concepts. By imaginatively examining this kinaesthetic or 'muscular' sense we would be adding a visual and motor dimension to what has been so far treated as an aural experience.

Above all, however, it is hoped that the detailed examination in this chapter of the three examples described, already will have begun to generate avenues for individual discovery, and to trigger 'connections' to other musical models in the reservoir of every music teacher's own musical resources.

3
Rhythm and Movement

WHAT IS RHYTHM?

To many musicians the word 'rhythm' often brings back emotional memories of childhood piano lessons, a relentless metronome and one's endeavours to 'keep in time'. This association with strictness or rigidity is probably counterbalanced by another image, that of the loose-limbed jazz player of the inimitable song *I Got Rhythm*, and in some contemporary compositions where rhythms unfold without pulse or metre.

Dictionary definitions emphasise the ordering and structuring function of the word yet the concept of rhythm is so vast that no one sentence can do it justice. Curt Sachs in *Rhythm and Tempo* (1953) offers a range of derivations such as *'flow'* (from Greek word rhythmos), *'movement and moderation'*, *'flux and dam'*, *'order of movement'* (Plato), and *'organisation of time in parts accessible to the senses'* (Heusler). More forceful, however, is his statement which forms the stimulus for this chapter:

'Rooted deep in physiological grounds as a function of our bodies, rhythm permeates melody, form and harmony, it becomes the driving and shaping force, indeed the very breath of music . . .' (page 11)

Rhythmic movement is best understood through physical movement. Too often, one feels that it is left to the teachers in primary schools to fully explore the muscular or Kinaesthetic* sense in expressing music through bodily movements and dance. For *rhythm* is *movement*, felt inwardly and expressed actively. This activity is seen in the body as we move and dance, chant

* Kinaesthetic — feeling of movement (Greek, *kinisis* — movement, *aesthesis* — feeling)

and sing, play an instrument, conduct and shape a musical performance.

In sum, rhythm is the *life force* of music, the power to transform a dull or mechanistic interpretation into a musically expressive and vital experience.

TAPPING THE RHYTHMIC POTENTIAL

Let us try to draw on the rhythmic possibilities of an easily learned American song — *Five Hundred Miles*

Imagining that we are going to teach this song to a group of twelve year old children, we realize that it should be presented in an easy flowing style. The melody and words can be easily assimilated. By first performing the song to ourselves, our 'inner performance' as it were, we will capture the nostalgic feelings portrayed and the easy swing of the tempo. The accompaniment will be light whether played on guitar or piano matching the swaying quality of the tempo. We might invite the children to 'finger-click' in time with the pulse. As left hand finger-clicks alternate with right there is a fair chance that bodies will sway from side to side 'one-two, one-two', reinforcing the expressive quality which we are hoping to encourage. This may lead on to determining the stronger, felt, accent of the two and suggestions invited for using alternative body percussion, eg thigh slapping, clapping, tapping, to express the strong/weak alternation.

The next step might focus on the recurrent rhythm pattern

of the melody ♫♫ , asking half the class to tap this while the other half keeps the pulse. This rhythm pattern could then be notated on the board or overhead projector together with any other patterns derived from the song.

viz. 1 ♫♩♫♫

2 ♩♩♩♩♩

3 ♩ ♩♩

Each of these patterns could then be practised in turn employing different hand and body sounds: they can be combined, played as a round, perhaps transferred to percussion instruments; in effect simple sight-reading in a game-like atmosphere.

Rhythm pattern 2 ♩♫ is an interesting example, so familiar that we often overlook its potential. It occurs frequently, as an ostinato, in a wide spectrum of musical styles and periods. The children could now be asked to identify which of the notated patterns appears in pieces based on this elemental rhythmic figure. We might have access to Grieg's *Wedding at Troldhaugen* for piano:

the *Padstow Song* (reproduced in full on pages 38-39)

or No. 3 of Lennox Berkeley's *Five Short Pieces for Piano*

If we have a selection of contrasting pieces to hand some fruitful exploration could be concerned with their differing expressive qualities. The common bond, ie ♪♫, far from imposing rigidity or sameness, is changed or transformed in every new context. The *Wedding at Troldhaugen*, for example, is a joyous, march-like, processional piece. One can perceive this, as our pupils are able to do, without the aid of verbal clues or title. Indeed it would be better to lead the class to discover these elements rather than to feed them with the title prematurely.

We might ask: what aspects of this piece contribute to its overall mood? Is it the springy accentuation on first and third beats? Is it reinforced by the way in which the melody often moves with the ostinato, quaver with quaver, giving it a precision and briskness? (see musical quotation, page 36). Is it the way in which the bass hops from deep to middle register, the dotted rhythm at the close of each phrase or is anything significant about the triplet decoration in the melody?

Whichever facets of this first section are highlighted, would we not agree that the 'bonding' quality of the overall rhythmic feeling is taut, as tight as a circus high wire.

The second example, the *Padstow Song*, performed every First of May in Padstow, Cornwall, is another processional piece celebrating the beginning of summer. Dancing exuberantly through the village streets, the Padstow people sing to the accompaniment of accordions and drums. A man dressed up as a horse ('Old Oss') is the central character who, during the course of the verses, every now and then sinks to the ground pretending to die. At the beginning of each chorus 'Unite and Unite' he jumps up again and the procession carries on its way. Why not push the tables and chairs out of the way and perform it? The song is hypnotically rhythmic and there is a 'follow-my-leader' quality as the dancers sing, clap and stamp to the music. Tambours, claves and tambourines would provide fitting accompaniment:

Padstow Song

Chorus Unite and unite
Now let us unite,
For summer is a-coming today.
And whither we are going
We all will unite
In the merry morning of May.

Verse 1 The young boys of Padstow
They might if they would,
For summer is a-coming today.
They might have made a ship
And gilded it with gold,
In the merry morning of May.

(Chorus: Unite and unite, etc)

Verse 2 The young girls of Padstow,
They might if they would,
For summer is a-coming today.
They might have made a garland

Of roses white and red
In the merry morning of May.

(Chorus)

Verse 3 Oh where are the young men,
That now would have danced,
For summer is a-coming today.
Oh some they are in England
And some they are in France
In the merry morning of May.

(Chorus)

This traditional song, this Cornish custom, may provide
pupils with sufficient clues to Grieg's inspirational source —
the rituals and customs embedded in the past and the measured
walk or tread (left, right, left, right, one-two, one-two) from
which *western* music derives its principles of rhythmic organisation.

What we find is that here the melody line is at one with the
ostinato. It appears to grow from it. The song is heavy, robust
and strong, stamped into the ground rather than springing
from it, the heaviness reinforced by the unexpected accentuation of normally weak beats.

viz

Yet in contrast, let us turn to our third example No. 3 of
Lennox Berkeley's *Five Short Pieces for Piano*. Here is the same
ostinato figure as before:

but how transformed is the effect. We could ask our pupils to listen a second time to the left hand alone, and make comparisons with our other examples. Will they not notice the harmonic richness of the latter? We would not expect a formal or technical analysis but it is highly likely that the bare or hollow quality of the open fifths in the Grieg and in the *Padstow Song* would be described in recognisable terms and compared with the fuller, chordal texture of Berkeley's music. They might also try to describe the dissonance brought about by the major second intervals which occur frequently throughout the piece. This example shares many similar features with Richard Rodney Bennett's *The Birds* (our example in chapter two). Again the melody soars and plummets giving the music a plaintive, nostalgic character, far removed from the driving, stamping quality of the *Padstow Song*.

Let us take now the simple ♪♫ ostinato common to all three quoted examples and begin to make connections with other works. One that springs instantly to mind is the second movement of Beethoven's *Seventh Symphony* which, we recall, begins with a sustained, though yielding, A minor second inversion chord (woodwind and horns) before the low strings introduce the theme:

Here is our, by now, familiar ostinato ♪♫. Like the *Padstow Song*, the melody and the ostinato form a harmonious whole; the melody appears to grow from the ostinato germ. Once again, our pupils could be led to listen purposefully, to make judgements about the quality of this particular musical encounter. How does this music sound? Is it heavy or light? Can we be more precise than this? Why do we think it sounds this way? What are the audible differences between this extract and the *Padstow Song*, for example?

Pursuing this idea of making connections let us refer again to the interesting feature of the *Padstow Song* (see pages 38-39) the accentuation of what is normally an unstressed beat: *Now* let us u-nite . . . *For* summer is a-coming today . . . . This leads us, in performance, to bend more strongly into the stepping movement, with a consequent prising off or upward spring on the next beat. A 'pop' song in the charts in 1980 shares this characteristic and could be explored along the same lines. The song is *Escape* (the Pina Colada Song) by Rupert Holmes where the rhythmic drive is provided by the bass.

and opens in this way.

As with many other 'folk' songs the *Padstow Song* is almost *hypnotically* rhythmic. Could it be that this driving rhythmic quality is part of what young people seek and find in 'pop' music, often described as the 'beat'? Another song from the 'pop' music charts, with the title *I am the Beat* shares a fundamental quality with our folk song example in its pounding drive and urgency.

PERCEPTION AND EXPRESSION

As an exercise let us imagine and then conduct the opening sections of each of our three original examples. The musical qualities perceived in Grieg's *Wedding at Troldhaugen*, would surely be expressed in movements of a fairly defined nature, showing contrasts between the bouncing accentuation of the first beat in the bass and the lightness of the second, third and fourth beats in each bar. On the other hand, one would feel and express a firmer, heavier two in a bar in the *Padstow Song*. Imagine then the pressing but gentle gestures inherent in the Berkeley *Piece No. 3* as the stronger first and third beats alternate with the weaker semi-staccato quavers on the alternating second and fourth.

Our thoughts on conducting are often so concerned with its functional role that we may overlook the fact that, despite the limitations of rostrum space, conducting is as *interpretive* and as *expressive* as dance. Head, facial features, shoulders, arms, wrists, legs, hips, the whole body is in constant motion within the close confines of a limited space. If we encourage our pupils to listen discriminately and lead them to reflect on the expressive and structural qualities in a varied musical repertoire, it would follow that we ask them to demonstrate these qualities. That is to say, having '*told*' how the music is, now '*show*' how! The confining space of a classroom does not preclude the activity of conducting and the many ideas which might spring from it such as listening and interpreting through gesture and posture (eg is the music outward going and positive or does it contract and fade?). Conductor's gestures could inspire instrumental work and group composition and there are occasions when class singing might be given additional momentum and purpose by asking the children to beat time expressively as they sing.

With some organisation, and possible collaboration with the PE staff for gymnasium space, why not develop these activities into movement and dance*. One such example has already been described (see page 38). As a custom or ritual the *Padstow Song* imposes its own discipline in a unified processional manner. Another similar example is to be found in Renouf and Smith's *Approach to Music Book 1, Round to the Left We Go* which is danced in a circle and based on the elemental ♩♫|♫♩ pattern. These dances would provide structured starting points before moving in to more abstract pieces where there is more scope for interpretation with consequently greater demands made on the individual's imagination.

How might we approach, for example, the *Farandole* from Bizet's *L'Arlésienne*, a movement based on two distinctive ideas?

Structurally our pupils would perceive that the strings begin with the theme (A) in unison before proceeding to play a 'follow-my-leader' game (canon). This is followed by a second contrasting idea (B) played by the flutes with tambourine accompaniment. The A theme returns, quickly interrupted by B, A once more, B joins in and there's a gradual crescendo with a final, accelerating statement of A and B together in the major mode.

Expressively they might describe theme A as firm and emphatic, strong rather than weak, taut rather than loose. Each beat is emphasised and the music has a spiky, detached quality. The flow seems controlled rather than free.

In contrast, theme B is light, more weightless in quality, more suspended with a feeling of pressing forward by the tambourine.

---

* In Norway and other Scandinavian countries it is assumed that accommodation for music in secondary schools automatically requires space large enough for folk music and dance.

At this point we can focus first on the opening theme A and then the contrasting B theme proceeding to experiment in movement and discover ways in which we might move to the music. These considerations might be helpful in guiding our work:

1 *How* should we move?
— in terms of *weight* (heavy or light)
  in terms of type of movement (sustained or detached)
— in terms of *time* (fast or slow)
— in terms of *flow* (free or controlled).
Much of this activity may have solved already the consideration of:

2 *Which* parts of our body should we move? Do we focus on our feet and the kind of movements they make (stepping, striding, running)? What of other parts of the anatomy — arms, shoulders, head, back, front, trunk? Do they move in unison, in turn, successively leading, or supporting? Does our body bend, twist or is it erect? If our legs and feet were stepping out the metrical rhythm (the time values of the rhythmic phrase) would the upper part of our body be interpreting the general flow of the music?
And then we could consider:

3 *Where* are we moving? How shall we use the space around us (personal space), general space, the shapes and pathways we make, the directions we take and the levels we use of height and depth?
And finally:

4 *Who with*? Do we dance alone, with a partner, in a group? If the latter how large is the group and what is the size and structure of the relationships within it?

This particular piece would appear to lend itself particularly to interpretation in pairs or groups with its canonic treatment and clearly contrasted themes.

For anyone who wishes to explore the potential of the dance dimension in greater depth, the authors would suggest that they read Emile Jaques-Dalcroze, *Rhythm, Music and Education* (1921 revised 1967) or Rudolf Laban's *Modern Educational Dance* (1948 revised 1963). As the former once said of music education through movement:
— its chief value lies in the fact that it trains the powers of apperception and of expression, and renders easier the externalisation of natural emotions.

It is hoped that the suggestions given will provide a stimulus for expression through music and dance. In this way, pupils may feel the muscular experience of expressing music, at the same time providing themselves and each other with a visual aid. They are, in fact, a visual representation of the music — a human score!

CONCEPTS OF METRE

If we were to look back at the musical examples quoted so far in this chapter, it would be noticeable that they are all in either duple or quadruple time. This has not been at all intentional but reinforces the fact that in 'Western' music the divisive 'strong/weak' pulsation is the norm. It has its basis in the way in which we walk, that is the left/right measured tread.

If, however, instead of this constant left/right alternation where the stress always falls on the same foot, we begin to group in threes: left/right/left — right/left/right the stress falls on first one then the other side of the body. The movement takes on a swaying quality; it becomes 'dance'. We can sense immediately a release from rigidity and a feeling of lightness and freedom in the additive rhythm of triple time. No matter which complexities of rhythm we work in, it is on the basis of 'twoness' and 'threeness' and their combinations that concepts of metric rhythm flow are based.

It would prove an interesting study in itself for us and our pupils' perception of pulse to concentrate on the aspect of 'twoness', 'threeness' and 'fourness', finding examples which are clear and unequivocal. We could then move from style to style, period to period, discovering where our conceptions broke down and the reason for it. For example, on searching through known materials and resources to hand we could purposely sift out 'three' time (or triple time) examples. There is the sea shanty *Spanish Ladies* for example, a song where definite working movements were made more tolerable by singing rhythmically (ex. 1). We also find the dance *Polonaise*, our example in Chapter Two with its unusually stressed third beats and the lilting chorale prelude *Jesu, Joy of Man's Desiring* where there is a feeling of three within three, a reinforcement of the dance like quality on account of the constantly flowing triplets (ex. 2). There is the song *The Returned Sailor* who, we are told, returns to his sweetheart in the month of May (ex. 3). Rural or Spring-like songs of this nature appear to be normally cast in triple time. It would appear that May (the month) has

a monopoly on triple time. For example there is the Elizabethan part-song *O Lusty May* by David Melvill (ex. 4) and
May is Come, a German folk-song and the only one in triple
time contained in a book of some twenty-two German 'Wander-
lied' (ex. 5).

Nor must we forget that the paradoxical nature of $\frac{6}{8}$ time (or
compound duple) is the result of its dance-like 'threeness'. Its
nature is heard either in jiggy sprightliness eg *For he's a jolly
good fellow* or in the swaying, swinging quality of boating songs
such as *Speed Bonny Boat* or *Row, Row, Row Your Boat*.

On the other hand there is an almost stressless flow in Elizabethan madrigals and 'ayres' where the natural cadence of the

spoken word dominates the flow, for example:

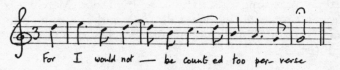

For I would not — be count ed too per-verse

in Thomas Campian's *So Quicke, So Hot, So Mad*
or

Can she ex-cuse my wrongs with vor—tues cloaks.

Shall I call her good when she proves un—kind.

in John Dowland's *Can She Excuse My Wrongs*.

The exploration of time concepts can be the focus for class-room composition. We might set assignments such as: first compose a fast piece with a heavy, driving quality in duple time, then devise a slow, floating piece of music in triple time. Songs could be composed with alternating sections in duple, triple or quadruple time. Experiments might also be made with conscious accentuation of normally weak accents or by gradu-ally pushing back the accentuation from first to second and subsequent beats either melodically or in ostinato accompani-ments.

Rhythmically Western music has confined itself very largely to units of two, three or four beats yet the combination of two and three to make 'five' time is far from being unusual and one which opens up a trail to the interesting area of 'irregular times'.

We could ask the class to point out what the following musi-cal examples have in common:

Tschaikovsky 6th Symphony - (2nd movement).

Holst Planets' (Mars)

From here we could proceed to explore Dave Brubeck's *Take 5* record compilation of many of his successful jazz ventures into irregular times such as the title piece itself, the $\frac{7}{4}$ *Unsquare Dance* and the $\frac{9}{4}$ *Blue Rondo a la Turk*. Lennox Berkeley's compositions *Five Short Pieces for Piano*, in addition to the example quoted earlier in this chapter, include one (No. 1) which in its seventeen bar length explores six different time signatures through nine changes, ie $\frac{7}{8} \frac{5}{8} \frac{6}{8} \frac{5}{8} \frac{3}{8} \frac{6}{8} \frac{7}{8} \frac{6}{8} \frac{4}{8}$.

As we move further east and south across the world there are the *Six Dances in Bulgarian rhythm* of Bela Bartok (*Mikrokosmos* Vol. VI) in the first of which he employs a time signature: $4 + \frac{2}{8} + 3$

which would particularly lend itself to movement as would de Falla's last movement from *El Amor Brujo*.

Apart from ways in which one can tap out these irregular rhythms as patterns on knees, desks or bongo drums, there is also potential in using circular formation. Standing side by side, palm to palm, the feeling for $4 + 2 + 3$ or $3 + 2 + 2$ can be sought and grasped by swaying side by side or by moving gently round tapping out the rhythm pattern with our feet.

And so we are beginning to move away from the even beats of such a large proportion of Western 'serious' music to, as it were, break out of a cultural straitjacket. Why not search out examples of *cross rhythms*, such as Rodrigo's *Concerto de Aranjuez* for guitar and orchestra which begins:

and Bernstein's *I Want to be in America* from West Side Story:

And of course we could create interesting *polyrhythms* by putting different times together. Here is one suggestion for a simple classroom experiment which could be carried out first by using different body sounds and then transferred to instruments.

Group one begins with a continuous stressed 1 in three, eg

Group two adds a continuous

Thus we have:

When this has been grasped and can be performed without difficulty a third group adds a melodic line:

*Note that on repeating Grp. 1 will play, in effect, one beat later than on first playing.

The American composer Steve Reich has expressed and demonstrated his interest in Eastern Music and his fascination for its complex polyrhythms. A most effective introduction to his music is *Clapping Music for Two Performers* in which the first performer keeps up a constant ostinato. The second performer begins in unison with the pattern being played twice. After this the latter begins his pattern successively one note later, on the second, the third, fourth and so on, until at variation thirteen the two players are back in unison again. (See below.)

It should now be obvious that the use of time signatures is at this point becoming more of a hindrance than a help. Our

Clapping Music for Two Performers — Steve Reich

accustomed feeling for regularity, for twoness and threeness has been obliterated as each note counts as a basic unit. Indian music could be approached from this point where rhythm is based on a basic rhythm pattern or cycle, a *Tala*. Many patterns are played or improvised against it to produce polyrhythms in a similar way to the last example.

Some music will free us from regular metre, in the way that Indian music does or Stravinsky in *The Soldier's Tale*. Sometimes even *pulse* is abandoned. For example, in Stockhausen's *Kontakte* we hear a spreading mass of sound followed by dramatic events — leaping, jagged, disconnected, surprising. There is no metre, no pulse; yet there is certainly *rhythm*. This music has its own kind of vitality and we could move and dance to its irregularities as easily as to a waltz or rock number. *Carré*, also by Stockhausen, is *seasonal* in its rhythmic life. Slow changes over a broad soundscape or cloudscape are heard as rhythmic change, but the change is more like Spring merging into Summer than a 'weak' beat before a 'strong'.

Further exploration of rhythm is beyond the scope of this book. We have, however, attempted to scratch the surface of a rich vein of music and to suggest ways in which it might be approached. By these means we may help to bring our pupils nearer to knowing the music by means of the neglected 'sixth sense'; in other words, through 'feeling it in our bones!'

4
Sounds into Music

SOUND AND MUSIC

Consider the fantastic range of sounds utilised by music. The entire vocal range of vowels and consonants found across the world, instruments that are shaken, blown, beaten or bowed, sounds that are electronically amplified, modified or generated: these uncountable sounds that have been pressed into service have no single characteristic that makes them in some way musical. Many sounds come to us with a strong sense of pitch, others impress us with their colour and timbre; there are sounds that are marked out by long or short durations and others which have a distinctive quality of loudness or softness. These are indeed the only dimensions of sound as we perceive it, four in all: pitch, timbre, duration, loudness. Out of such materials music is made. The possibilities are infinite.

Because music has been made from such a vast spectrum of sound possibilities and because there seems to be no limit imposed on the kinds of sounds that, at different times and in different places, have been recognised as having musical potential, we are led to the inevitable conclusion that *any* sound can be invested with musical properties. However, we should not fall into the error of supposing that sound in some way automatically becomes music. Spoken language, for example, involves sound and is not music. Indeed, we tend to ignore the sound of speech in order to concentrate on the meaning. If we do become more aware of word sounds, say by repeating a word over and over again, the meaning tends to disappear altogether. The same thing can happen when we are listening to people with a regional accent that we happen to find unusual, or friends who have particular vocal mannerisms or attractive qualities of speech. The sound of *speech* itself can be so fascinating that we may miss a good deal of what is actually being said in *language*, the meaning which is invested in the sounds. Almost the opposite is true of music. Our attention here is directed towards the 'musical' behaviour of sound. Sound in music and sound in spoken language require different mental attitudes if we are to make sense of them. Our way of listening is different. To take another example, we also have different ways of dealing with music and 'noise'. Noise is simply unwanted sound; sound that is distracting us from attending to sounds that *are* wanted. A lot of noise actually starts off as music on radios or record-players, and here again we become aware that the difference between noise and music is mainly psychological, it depends upon a mental set or attitude. One man's music can easily become another's noise. Sound is not music until it is regarded in a special way.

All this may seem unnecessary as a preliminary to an essentially 'practical' chapter. Unfortunately though there has been a fair amount of confusion about the relationship of sound to music that has, in some cases, distorted classroom practice. 'Sound' became an 'in' word in the 'seventies. We all came into contact with books bearing titles such as *New Sounds in Class*, *Sound and Silence*, *Exploring Sound*, *Sounds Fun*. Often the principles and activities advocated went beyond mere sound and it was usually recognised that something important has to happen to sound, at least in the imagination, before we are engaged with music. Indeed, *Sound and Silence* (Paynter and Aston (1970) must be one of the most imaginative and influential books in the field of music education. However, the idea that sound is synonymous with music was sown in people's minds and some teaching was influenced in an undesirable way, where making lists of sounds, inventing new sounds, identifying different sounds, or mechanically making sounds became important activities that sometimes (though not always) went no further. It was, of course an attempt to begin again, to make a new start, without the clutter of inherited classical tradition about our ears, without limited preconceptions as to what counts as music, and without an inhibiting emphasis on a range of skills and knowledge that are ill-suited to the classroom today and are alien to many pupils. The 'new' focus on sounds, centring on contemporary music, was and is both necessary and important but it needs placing into a perspective. We can do this by remembering that *music is a special way with sounds*. In music, sounds are perceived to be in coherent relationships with each other: they are also perceived as having particular qualities of feeling, they appear to have a kind of character, to exude a particular mood or atmosphere, or to make certain kinds of gestures.

In Chapter One we described these coherent relationships as the 'structure of music' and the qualities of feeling we called 'expressive character'. Only when the materials of raw sound are transformed by psychological processes in the mind of composers or performers or audience does music really begin. And only then is it possible to find delight or, on occasion, be profoundly moved. The manipulation of sound itself may involve a whole gamut of skills (knowing *how*) and the science of acoustics (knowing *that*) may give us certain kinds of useful information. But the sounds themselves will only speak as music when these skills and this knowledge serve particular structural and expressive purposes (knowing *it*) and thus make possible the satisfaction and active pleasure of responding according to our personal value systems (knowing *what's what*).

In this chapter we shall explore some of the possibilities that arise and can be discovered on the borderland between sound and music, keeping a special watch on the development of structural and expressive elements. We shall certainly not want to linger too long in the musically barren territory of sound as such but move as far into the domain of music as we can.

REPETITION AND CONTRAST

One of the most obvious and fundamental ways of imposing order upon sound, of creating a sense of structure, is the device of *repetition*. We could say that all musical forms, no matter in what style or at what level of complexity, are evolved from repetition and its necessary corollary — *contrast*. Repetition is found under many names, such as ostinato, motif, beat, figure or theme. Likewise contrast is sometimes identified under such labels as variation, modulation, development or transposition.*

Let us look at one example of the device of repetition and the effect of contrast. It is strikingly managed in a once popular reggae song *This is Reggae Music*. Very roughly, the first part could be rendered in notation. We know that it is impossible to transmit in notation the actual quality of any music, let alone in this particular style, but the following may serve as a guide. Ultimately only listening to or imagining a performance

* See chapter 1, page 10.

will give any idea of the character of this particular song, especially the vocal ornamentation.

This is Reggae Music — Zap Pow

We notice the repeated rhythmic figure on the 'high-hat'
cymbal, the ubiquitous chord of G minor and the 8-times
repeated ostinato in the bass. We recognise that the vocal line
is made mainly from a repeated phrase and that the entry of the
brass emphasises (toward the end) the persistence of the G
minor chord. Where then are the changes or contrasts? We now
notice that the vocal phrases are not mere repetitions but have
subtle variations through inflection of pitch and rhythm. No
two 'repetitions' are exactly the same. We become aware of
changes in the level of loudness and in the instrumentation after
the 26th bar. But perhaps the most obvious thing that strikes
us, the most powerful break into a repeated event, is the move
to the F major chord after 33 bars. The effect of this is at once
to surprise and delight us. This is only achieved because our
expectations have been aroused — by about bar 30 we are
waiting for comething to happen, we long for a strong contrast.

These are some of the structural properties. We have still to
tease out the expressive character. There are general things to
be perceived — the confident, bright rhythms, the spare, clear

textures that contribute towards an impression of tightness and sharp image. There are more specific qualities. The song opens with a characteristic reggae drum flourish, surely a device to catch our attention and impress us with a sense of purpose. 'Here we go, hold on!' it seems to say. Then there is the 'serious' character of the unchanging minor harmony, the light but forward-pushing cymbal rhythms and the weight of the crescendo, the bite of the brass and the powerful sense of expansive arrival when the harmony ultimately shifts.

Now, of course, we know that words cannot convey what really happens in music. Performers and composers themselves may not be able to articulate helpfully in any other way than through performance. But if we are *teaching* music, what then? We surely need to be aware of these kind of events inside music which make the experience worth having. We also need to evolve a language to enable us to share musical discoveries with others. Let us be quite clear: any person who is not perceiving some of the elements we have discovered in this song can in no sense be 'appreciating' it. We shall find it very hard to know whether or not musical perception is at work unless some kind of conversation takes place.

It may be thought that it is hardly necessary to tease out these musical elements from a popular song. Does not the media already see that people come to know 'it' well enough? The answer is probably no. The media sees to it that we *overhear* a lot of music, not that we really *listen*. The most typical reactions to a pop song are 'I like it' or 'It's rubbish', hardly evidence that much attention is given to what is happening *inside* the song. This is the teacher's job.

PAIRS OF SOUNDS

So how might we help pupils to make these kinds of discovery? We have been especially concerned with the simplest form of direct repetition which dissolves into a single, striking contrast. It is fairly easy to organise activities which involve the exploration of possibilities here. Pupils might work in pairs with two contrasting sounds, one sound each. Hand sounds, voice sounds and 'furniture' sounds may all serve along with more conventional instrumental sounds. One sound is to be repeated until it seems essential to break the repetition with the second chosen sound. The roles can then be reversed. Some discussion will become necessary. Does the change tend to come more quickly if the repetitions are quicker? Is it possible to make an interesting piece by repetition of some aspect of sound, say its pitch or timbre, but to get some contrast by changing say, its loudness or spacing in time? In this way we might be able to make a longer passage before we feel the need to bring in the second sound. In order to prevent this activity from becoming just an exercise in construction we might want to suggest that each pair chooses to develop a particular expressive character, perhaps a relationship between the two sounds as if they were angry, spooky, peaceful or machine-like. We become aware of the way in which the sounds relate. A sound can interrupt another, join in with it, echo, mimic, be completely different, appear tentative or shocking. It may be yielding, dogmatic, hard or soft, all in relationship with other sounds. (These qualities are all relative beyond the fairly obvious character of very loud or soft, harsh, slow or fast sounds.)

Vocal sounds are particularly effective in this kind of activity. Single syllables or mere vowels and consonants are a rich source of contrasting sounds and they are fairly easy to handle. An unvoiced 'p' or 't' is strikingly different from a hummed 'm' or a long 's' or 'sh' and the small-scale of the sounds makes composition in pairs a real possibility without producing too much clamour in the room. The important thing is to concentrate on a few sounds, perhaps only two, and develop a short piece from them that has some shape and direction and a clear expressive quality.

RELATED POSSIBILITIES
Many professionally recorded compositions can be approached through and illuminated by this kind of activity. We have already discussed one of them, discovered in the idiom of reggae. It may be possible to explore *Prelude* from *Cantos de España* by Albeniz which can be heard on piano or guitar. This is surprisingly close in 'feel' to *This is Reggae Music*. Again, in G minor we have an ostinato — or is it?

If we really listen we shall hear that although each four-bar phrase has the same urgent rhythm and a similar melodic

curve there are differences and they occur especially in the
3rd and 4th bars of the phrases. Other contrasts are effected
by the increasingly hard accents at the start of each bar, by a
sustained crescendo, by a thickening of texture and changes in
register and eventually by a very high 'bright' (D major) chord.
How much of this can people perceive? Far more than is often
assumed, given the chance to listen and discuss and without
being diverted by knowing 'that' Albeniz was born in 1860 or
'that' there are four other pieces in Opus 232 or 'that' *Prelude*
is in ternary form. There is indeed a middle section, quite different in expressive character. (The beginning of it has been described by one school group with their teacher as 'floating and
meeting'.) But to begin with, the idea of ternary form is too
general and unspecific. We should first become aware of the
feeling of urgency and energy, achieved mainly through accent,
speed and crescendo.

A similar idea could be the basis for group improvisation. An
ostinato might be:

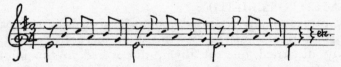

In the fourth bar someone might contribute a contrasting idea,
something like:

Accents could appear in different places on non-tuned percussion instruments, melodies can be made to float over the top
in a more serene way:

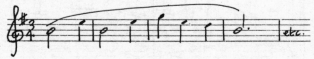

Middle sections of quite a different character can be tried out in and played by small groups to see which of them make a good contrast to the first part, and to find ways of linking sections. In these ways, (as composers, performers and in audience) music is being penetrated, understood, taken into childrens' experience.

So many possibilities present themselves when thinking in this way. Activities with repeated sounds may help us to understand something of the Fourth of the *Nine Piano Pieces* by Stockhausen where the chord

is repeated 139 times (ff–pppp) and then a further 87 times before other musical elements intervene with a longed-for contrast. Words and bits of words are the basic materials for Stockhausen's *Stimmung* and a single held chord is its predominant 'repetition'. Berio's *Sequenza III* explores an incredible range of vocal sound. It is interesting to notice that he gives 46 different indications of expressive character from 'accusing' and 'urgent' to 'wistful' and 'witty'. Part of Berio's *Visage* opens up the possibility of identifying the feelings (expressive character) through which the 'singer' passes in reaction to the electronic sounds.

But even to begin to list musical works in this way goes against the grain of our principles. We are not interested in *using* music to illustrate some general point, such as the range of vocal sounds or the use of single chords, but in working into and around an individual piece (knowing it). These few suggestions are only included to show how, once started in this way, there are multiple possibilities depending on what resources are available and what seems likely with particular groups in specific schools.

SILENCE
Corilan Overture — Beethoven (the beginning)

Silence can be electrifying, especially when it is broken into by great wedges of sound. Silence can be one of the most extreme forms of contrast, almost shocking in impact. Another obvious instance is the ending of Sibelius's *Fifth Symphony* which is just as striking in its way as the start of *Corilan* and seems even more jagged or craggy because of the irregular spacing in time of the massive orchestral chords. Passages like these are so dramatic and so obvious in effect that they would make a good beginning to an exploration of silence as one of the materials of music. We know how the 'meaning' of silence can change in everyday conversation. A silence after an insulting remark is different from a silence that follows very bad news, or silence that signifies incomprehension of what is said; and these are all quite different silences from the split-second of quietness between the telling of a joke and someone 'getting it'. There are dramatic silences like those made by Beethoven and Sibelius, delicate silences etched with sprigs of sound as in a quiet country place, ominous silences before a storm, silences that generate in us a strong sense of expectation — surely something has to happen. The ending of the *Kyrie* in Mozart's *Requiem* has such a silence. We know *something* must happen, the great weight of sound needs to come properly to rest, the tensions of that massive discord before the pause *must* be resolved (see below)

There are many group activities that enable us to explore the possibilities of silence in music. Let us consider just one of them. After discussing different types of silence, three or four

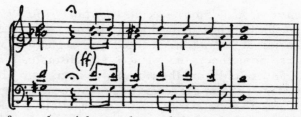

groups of people might work out how to lead into a particular silence 'feeling'. For example, a silence approached abruptly after a hectic burst of sound will feel very different from a silence which gently emerges out of a long diminuendo, or a silence which is not quite absolute but has a ghost of a sound left resonating in it. One group may work on making an abrupt or startling silence, as though suddenly a light were turned off; another group may prepare for a silence that gradually steals up on us, a third group could build up sporadic silences, little bursts of sound separated by patches of silence. Once again we are engaged in the act of composition. Now we can have mini-performances, one group to the others, (in audience) and discussion as to the effectiveness of what was done. We might now try to make a longer composition using all of the groups and deciding on the best order of events to make an interesting structure and relating the different expressive qualities. For example, it may be that it is decided to start with the attention-claiming, startling silence which probably requires a fairly high level of loudness and a busy texture beforehand. This may be repeated to increase a feeling of assertiveness and be followed by a longer passage of sporadic silence, perhaps conveying a feeling of uncertainty and anxiety. This whole sequence may be repeated, giving way at the end to the long diminuendo into the almost imperceptible silence. We may or may not need to notate this, but it would be helpful to record it for subsequent listening and discussion. 'Trying it out' is the only way to be sure.

From this kind of basis we might now give some attention to another composition from the professional area of music. In fact this work has been in our minds when developing the activities so far and some of the ideas for practical work have been stimulated by it. (Notice the sequence here. We did not begin with general ideas and search for examples but abstracted the general from the particular music.) Beethoven and Sibelius were helpful and so is Boulez. One movement of *Le Marteau sans Maitre*, the fourth movement entitled

Commentaire II de 'Bourreaux de Solitude' (*the 'Hangman of Solitude'*), depends radically on silence. We hear hard, brittle flurries of sound, fragmented and separated by long-ish silences. Sometimes the silences are absolute, but often a high or a low sound from the vibraphone lingers on. The start-stop character of the music seems to communicate uncertainty, anxiety. Later the viola tries to establish a more confident, sustained line of sound, but temple-bells summon up more bursts of activity until a final silence appears to leave us expect-ing something, waiting for we know not what. All this surely makes more sense if we have ourselves worked with silence and fashioned music from it. So too would the third movement of *Et Expecto Resurrectionem* by Messiaen, where silences are employed in a bold way to mark off strikingly different musical ideas — shrill woodwind, tubular bells, and violent crescendos. This music is so dramatic as to almost compel attention. In this silence plays its own special part.

It must be stressed that these are only examples of a *pro-cedure*, a way of generating worthwhile activities from our own musical experience. Better instances and more imaginative classroom work will surely be developed by others in their own particular context. We ought also to remind ourselves that differences of musical style are not to be seen as obstacles but as instances of the richness of the world of music. In the fairly simple classroom activities discussed above it will not matter if the compositions are metric and tonal, atonal, or rooted in reggae. What does matter is the internal consistency of what is done and the development of skills, concepts, musical perceptions and positive attitudes towards music.

SETS OF SOUNDS
Because single sounds by themselves have little potential as music and therefore depend on relationships with other sounds, and because the human mind has a tendency to seek for order and look for these relationships, it is not really surprising that conventional groupings of sounds have emerged at all stages of musical development. Sometimes these groupings, or sets of sounds, have become fundamental to a particular style or even to several styles. The sets we know as major and minor scales are a particularly obvious example. We do know, however, that other sets may serve us just as well, including modes, pentatonic and whole-tone scales, note-rows, râgas and even tunes when, for example, in jazz they serve as a kind of row,

to be varied in almost any way except in actual serial order. Certain harmonic progressions also can be regarded as sets, for example the customary IV, V, I and the 12-bar blues progression. Sometimes musicians take or make a small set to act as a limiting factor in composition or improvisation. Such limitations are essential at times to 'get us going' and to help with the problems of relating sounds in a consistent way. For example, Debussy has a prelude for piano called *Les Tierces Alternées* (Book 2). Here only the interval of the third is used, as a set, and out of it a surprising number of different expressive qualities are generated. In the second of six *Kleine Klavierstuck* (Opus 19), Arnold Schoenberg also seems to be using thirds as a set and particularly the interval of B/G. Bartok is particularly fond of working from sets, sometimes rhythmic ostinati, sometimes interval sets of thirds, fifths, sixths and even sevenths, as we can find in *Game of Pairs*, the 2nd movement of *Concerto for Orchestra*. For obvious educational reasons he works with sets in his *Mikrokosmos*, 'fifth chords', 'triplets in 9/8 time', and so on. Sets are indeed valuable to teachers of music. They enable us to restrict technical difficulties and focus on a particular skill, they sharpen up aural discriminations through the perception of particular groups of related sounds; above all they provide a way of getting us started at a level further on than the mere manipulation of individual sounds. Sets have built-in relationships and sometimes expressive associations, as is the case with minor scales, Indian râgas and blues progressions.

We shall look briefly at just two familiar sets to establish ways of working with them.

DRONES AND ROWS

We are all familiar with drones in Scottish bagpipe music, though not everyone is fond of that particular sound. The device of a single (sometimes double or triple) held or repeated note against which more mobile and contrasting sounds come and go is by no means limited to Scotland. Bagpipes themselves seem to have existed in most European countries and there is a long tradition in Northumbria, France (Musette), Italy (Cornemuse) and Germany (Dudelsack). But the principle itself, that of a steady pitch allied to a flexible series of pitched sounds has been identified in the ancient world, in all kinds of folk and tribal music, in Arab countries, in Indian râgas, in popular music and in many compositions by composers in the western world where it is sometimes given the name of 'pedal'.

The widespread use of musical sets made of drones and rows of notes is understandable. There need be no great technical complexity, yet there are infinite possibilities of exploring the tensions and relationships between the still, fixed pitch and the associated row. Repetition and contrast are here very clearly identified.

To take a by now familiar and simple example, the bass G of *This is Reggae Music* (along with the other notes of the G minor triad), functions as a drone. The singer uses a row of only four notes over 32 bars, though we have already noticed the vocal ornamentation around these notes. What happens if we establish this one or two note drone and explore for ourselves the same row against it?

If this is done fairly slowly we shall become aware of a degree of tension associated with the note A and the 'coming home' feeling relating to G or possibly to D. Faster and 'swung' popular tunes can be invented using this set. The drone itself might be rhythmically articulated, syncopated.

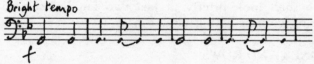

Explorations in free rhythm may come to resemble some aspects of Indian râgas. A râga is fundamentally, though not entirely, a mode or row, often with differences depending on whether or not it is in an ascending or descending pattern, but it is not simply a kind of scale. If one sound is emphasised rather than another in relation to the drone, or if notes are approached in different ways, perhaps by a leap or step, then the whole character of the râga is changed. However, for our purposes we may notice that improvised ragas are very much ways of exploring the possibilities of drones and rows. Unfortunately they are impossible to notate adequately and therefore to instance on paper. It is worth spending some time listening to the râga improvisations of artists like Ravi Shankar.

It does not take very long to realise that the first part of an improvisation (the âlâp) seems to be mapping out the shape of the râga, establishing a relationship with the drone. There can be real delight in allowing oneself to be teased by the player, who often refuses to return to the drone pitch for long periods of time and by this delay arouses a strong sense of expectation. When the return is achieved we experience (if we have been attentive auditors) a release of tension, a feeling of arrival. The structure of the âlâp is woven out of these relationships between drone and melody. The expressive character, on the other hand, is partly determined by the intervals of a râga but also in India by association with times of day, or particular festivals or moods. For example, the basis of the *Râga Vibhasa* is (roughly):

The associated mood is loveliness or beauty.

The *Râga Durga* signifies joy and energy and has this structure:

This is obviously a version of the more common pentatonic scale and the distribution of the intervals *is* different in expressive quality from the first example, the *Râga Vibhasa*.

It is not difficult to organise activities along these lines. Many pupils can be employed humming drones, keeping the sound going by breathing at different times. At the same time they will be listening to the râga played on a xylophone, or recorder or melodica or any melody instrument. The player simply plays the râga series in order, up and down — so much, for now, is pre-determined. The freedom to discover possibilities lie in choosing speeds, the time between and lengths of notes, levels of loudness, whether notes are repeated or not, whether played smoothly or detached. Later the notes can be taken out of series and used in any order. Once the pitch relationships are familiar to the ear the sequencing of order becomes a real choice, not accidental and arbitrary. Four or five groups could take different râga series and compose, eventually perform and be in audience to the other groups. We have no need to use authentic râgas. Any row will serve. There are quite different expressive possibilities to be explored from rows such as this.

The first note may serve as a drone, but what happens if we choose others? How would it sound if we changed from drone to drone?

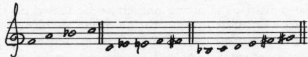

The last of these is of course a whole-tone scale, sometimes used by Debussy and Ravel. (Perhaps we should make it clear that we are using the term 'row' in a general sense to sets of pitches. Atonal note-rows would be special instances of these.)

The apparent impenetrability of Indian music and even the slightly more abrasive sound of bagpipes become more accessible to the understanding if we engage in hearing for *ourselves* what happens between drone and melodies. For example, the *Râga Kendara* played on reed instruments (shannai) and recorded for Volume One of the *History of Music in Sound* leaps out of the confusing and dull context of mere musical history and becomes a game of 'touch and run' between drone and melody row. How many times does the melody 'touch' the drone in the first passage? Let the pupils find out — it not only helps to develop aural skills but is a way of discovery, exploring what makes this music exciting, meaningful, worth knowing. We surely violate music if we use it as an example of a 'style' and for no other reason. Every piece that is played must be helped to speak for itself. The teacher's job is to prepare the ground in such a way that any negative attitude — 'Indian music, so what?' — is just not given much of a chance. Going beyond this we may also be opening up possibilities for the development of certain individuals as composers and performers themselves, extending the range of skills and sensitivity and helping to widen the repertoire of devices and procedures that, for the composer at least, are essential for freedom. There is no prison so restrictive as ignorance.

FURTHER POSSIBILITIES

SOUNDS INTO MUSIC   69

We know this music as a tranquil and relatively uneventful passage in the glorious *Messiah*. Yet, taken by itself it has its own scale of structural tensions and a very special expressive character. Much of it could easily be adapted for classroom performance and the idea of alternating between a tonic and dominant drone could serve as a basis for group compositions along with the row that Handel uses.

Look out too for pieces called *Musette* (bagpipes) in dance suites by Bach and his contemporaries.

A striking way to begin a movement is with a drone by itself. Brahms does this with a double drone at the beginning of his *Serenade in D Major*, Opus 11.

Now the drone has moved and at this change the clarinet takes up the melody. Soon the drone shifts downwards in step as the orchestral sound piles up and the activity multiplies. Are we aware of the brazen declaration (horns and trumpets, *ff*) over the original drone, amplified by violin trills on A? (bar 67) What began as a delicate and charming idea has become a massive weight of sound.

Even more massive and overwhelming is the single and unchanging drone on D that underpins *But the righteous souls are in the hand of God* in Brahms' *Requiem*. The trombones and others work in shifts to keep the D going while the noise and frantic business of the voices and other instruments drive the music on and on to the great concluding D major chord. The righteous souls are now surely out of reach of all that strife, gathered up into the eternal D!

A final instance might be from Tchaikovsky — the *Arabian Dance* from the *Nutcracker Suite*. Here is an articulated drone, unchanging for ages, making a strangely pulsating movement over which delicate woodwind sounds weave smooth lines. Before many bars have passed sets of thirds present a song-like expressive element. Can we work with thirds over variously articulated drones?

Instead of treating this music as a patch of general 'atmosphere' can we not penetrate it more by identifying the stiff repetition of the drone and hear it against the fluid melodies? Are we conscious of the richness of the sound when the drone gives way to other harmonies? Do our pupils notice that there is *any* kind of change at all? If not, then very little appreciation can be going on. If so, then a fund of experience is being acquired that will enrich contacts with other music, no matter what style, period or social and ethnic origin.

HORN CALLS

It may seem strange to call horn calls musical sets, but they are a particularly conventional way of grouping sounds into pairs. We know that the valveless horn (and trumpet) was unable to play every note of the scale, especially in the lower registers. Consequently the second horn had to leap about over the missing notes while the first horn generally managed to play stepwise passages. So the set

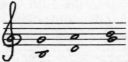

became very common and permeates the music of Haydn, Mozart and Beethoven, among others.

This particular set of notes has interesting classroom possibilities. Pupils might work in pairs or groups of six. Pitched 'keyboard' instruments — chime bars are ideal — can be laid out thus with the players on each side. We could have one player to three notes or one player to each note.

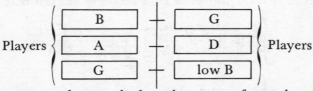

There are two rules attached to these sets of sounds: opposite sounds must always be played together (the pair of horns convention) and sounds in the same (vertical) row may only be played one at a time. Given these rules and these sounds, can the group or pair of players make interesting music? Each side can take turns to lead and the opposite player has then to follow. Remember, although the sounds are restricted by their number and by the rules, there is freedom to choose speeds, levels of loudness and order of sounds. Some groups might be given horn call sets in other keys — say D and C, or perhaps G minor. When each group has eventually performed its piece we could try to sequence them into a more extended piece with different key centres, and of course different themes and expressive characters; perhaps a Rondo? The availability of some orchestral instruments would transform the possibilities here. There is also the availability of a more extended set in the horn call tradition, should a group be able and interested to try to use it.

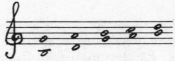

This experience of handling horn call figures will illuminate many classical and romantic works. For example, the start of the second movement of Beethoven's *Violin Concerto* has horn calls hidden in string chorus. We first hear them exposed and actually played on horns in the 10th bar, while the solo violin decorates them with light drops of sound.

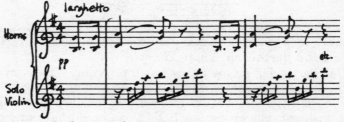

The second theme of the Rondo has straightforward horn calls played first on horns but later on oboe and clarinet.

Horn calls often seem to give to music an outdoor character, partly due, no doubt, to the open spacing in the underneath part but also because of the long association with hunting. Horn tone seems particularly rich in associations, evoking qualities relating to woods and fields, battlegrounds and, above all, a haunting sense of distance and the past. For young people to appreciate these qualities in *Des Knaben Wunderhorn* (Mahler) would require some degree of maturity and sensitivity, but if we never try we shall never know.

In particular, the song *Where the proud trumpets blow* is woven from haunting horn calls on many instruments in major and minor keys. The girl in the song is losing her lover to the war, to the 'green heath where the proud trumpets blow'. It would be a significant achievement to make it possible for pupils to perceive the expressive qualities here, and our guess is that it will be more likely if sets of horn calls have become part of the aural furniture of our classes. (In the same work, the song 'Comfort in misfortune' is much more extrovert with bold, unmistakeable horn calls.)

There are an infinite number of sound sets that have not been considered here, including those generated or modified electronically. We have chosen some of the obvious and practical ones. Whatever the source though, and whatever the level of technical complexity required to handle the sounds, the same principles hold. Sounds need to be perceived as relating to each other and as holding expressive qualities. Mere manipulation of sound is not helpful to musical development unless put to use for structural and expressive purposes.

It might be possible to generate an entire music curriculum from the basic fuel of exploring repetition and contrast along with discovering and using sets of sound. However this might be, there is no doubt, were it done well that young people leaving school would go into a world better equipped to find rich experiences in music.

5
Notations

In the long tradition of Western music, notation of one kind or another has been seen as an essential tool of composers and performers. We even use the same word, 'music', to describe the way things actually sound *and* the printed signs on paper. We must remember, however, that much of the world's music is not written down, for example, Indian music, jazz, a great deal of popular music, and all kinds of folk music. Notation is by no means an indispensable feature of a musical culture. In this century we have seen the evolution of a whole range of new notations, sometimes measured out in time by minute or second, often taking a graphic form. We have to bear these things in mind in order to avoid jumping to the conclusion that standard staff notation is in some way 'basic' to music.

We shall adopt a fairly broad definition of what a notation is. The following may serve reasonably well: *notation is a device representing some aspects of music*. The important word here is *some*. No notation can tell us all that we need to know. A great deal of information is transmitted through aural experience, even the highly developed form of staff notation relies on tradition and interpretation. As we all know, music is not played from notation in an automatic way and it can indeed be quite distressing to hear such a 'performance' where mechanical and translative accuracy is obvious but where there is no sense of style, line, phrase or structure, let alone expressive quality. It can be amusing to listen to a mechanical organ where the notation is a series of holes in a paper roll and the sound is usually incredibly 'wooden' in its precision. The effect is similar to an orchestra playing a Viennese Waltz *without* anticipating the second beat. The multitude of small but important decisions about the way we move from sound to sound, relatively small gradations of loudness and softness, and micro-second placing of sounds in time can never be fully indicated in any notation, yet they lie at the heart of music.

PROBLEMS AND POSSIBILITIES

Notation has problems, not least of which is the substantial element of skill and experience involved in its coding and de-coding. A good deal of instrumental teaching seems to go wrong when this set of skills is superimposed on technical problems. The recognition of this difficulty occurs in the violin teaching method of Suzuki, where notation is not introduced in the early stages and attention is focussed on aural experience (really listening) and the muscular 'feel' of playing the violin. Using a notation before aural and technical skills are developed can cause loss of spontaneity, musical insensitivity, 'barking at print'. Sometimes the visual aspect takes over and this, com-bined with a set of memorised rules, produces the sort of un-musical behaviour that is sometimes exemplified in GCE exami-nation scripts. But notation is, or ought to be, a helpful tool, not an impediment.

Notations have many positive possibilities and have been developed to help us to handle musical ideas as composer, per-former, or to direct our attention when we are in audience to music. They pin down music outside of time, functioning as a form of memory. We are able to build, perform and under-stand large-scale works without losing the thread of what has gone before, to construct complex textures perhaps employing large forces of musicians. Notation makes it possible to organise group work, even if the forces are many and varied as is the case with a band or orchestra. Imagine what would happen if a choral conductor or orchestral conductor had to teach every part by rote!

THE EDUCATIONAL VALUE OF NOTATIONS

Although 'looking at' can never replace 'listening to' in the centre of musical experience, there are times when the analogous properties between a notation and music itself may illuminate the work in hand. For example, to be able to visually follow the shape of a melody in a busy texture might help us to con-serve its shape when there is a tangle of accompanying figura-tion. Even the most sophisticated and developed musician is sometimes surprised to find details in complex scores that may initially have escaped the ear.

Above all, notations are useful to music education because they help to focus *attention*. Music is ephemeral and fleeting, many different things may happen in quick succession or simultaneously. The behaviour of music itself, along the four dimensions of pitch, timbre, duration and loudness, and the concepts that arise from these such as register, texture, sequence, repetition and contrast, can be highlighted to some extent with the help of notation. If notations can help us to examine the elements of music a little more carefully and thus enhance our perception and appreciation then they are of great value. On the other hand, if a notation seems to get in the way of direct musical experience it ought to be abandoned immediately. In the final analysis music works in sound whether heard or imagined.

Taking our broad definition of notation as a device representing *some* aspects of music, we can now explore some of the possibilities.

VERBAL DESCRIPTION

It may seem strange to include verbal description as a form of notation, but it really is. Considerable emphasis is placed on verbal notations of music, such as those in programme notes or reviews of concerts. Some people seem to think that such a description is helpful if not essential for understanding the piece that is being played. We are all familiar with the most common examples of 'programme music' and many teachers feel that music with a programme is somehow more approachable than music which is, so to speak, absolute or pure. This is certainly questionable but if we for the moment accept that words can sometimes help us to get further into music then it may be worth considering what kind of description is helpful and when it is not. In an article in *The Times* by Bernard Levin, *Notes on a programme for obscurity*, we are asked to consider this extract from a programme note:

' . . . *the adagietto functions to some extent as an introduction — in the present case to a predominantly linear, stratified Rondo-Finale of immense scope in which the structural parameters of sonata-rondo and variation are combined with a masterful display of fugal and imitative texturing worthy of late Beethoven . . .* '

This is describing music by Mahler. In the same programme

notes Levin draws our attention to a description of Schoenberg's
Piano Concerto which contains this passage:

'. . . *in the '40's Schoenberg reinterpreted this trait in harmonic rather than textural terms, contrasting instead the anti-
gravitational equality of serialism with the gravitational inequal-
ity of diatonicism.'*

Levin finds this unhelpful and contrasts it with a passage describing the slow movement of Beethoven's *Second Symphony* by
Rosa Newmarch:

*'The long slow movement (Larghetto) is happily designed to
contrast with the virile energy of the allegro. The strings start
with a melody of eight bars re-echoed by the woodwind. The
character of the theme is melancholy but tender rather than
poignant. The second subject (also eight bars) is treated in the
same way as the first by the strings and woodwind. A syncopated melody for the first violins seems to be leading us away
from the restrained sadness of the opening theme, and presently
the second violins and 'cellos bring in a new figure, distinctly
cheerful in character'.*

Levin suggests that the simplicity and honesty of the style
of writing here may enable us to recognise the music from the
description which is more than we can say for the first two
examples. We might notice that these earlier accounts seem to
be pre-occupied with what we have called Literature Studies
or Information, that is to say we are in a world of technical description, of stylistic background and historical development, while the Newmarch account of Beethoven's *Second
Symphony* confronts us with some of the structural and expressive elements of the work itself. Words like 'long', 'contrast', 're-echoed', 'leading us away', have to do mainly with
structural elements. Words such as 'slow', 'virile energy',
'melancholy', 'tender', 'restrained sadness' and 'cheerful' are
expressive elements perceived in this work. Any description
which fails to draw our attention to these qualities is likely to
be unhelpful; our experience of the music itself will remain
unilluminated by the description. Good teaching, like good
criticism, also relies on imagination, insight and sensitivity
with words, and the same fundamental question needs to be
asked: does what is said or written take us further into direct
experience of music? Does notation in words help?

WORDS AND MUSIC

Sometimes words are essentially interwoven with music, as in songs, opera, oratorio. The meaning of these words has some strong connection with the music, and in classroom rehearsals and performances we ought to be discovering something of these relationships. We might ask questions. Is there a particular or important word? Does the music help to emphasize its importance, perhaps by making a note longer or louder? Ought we to emphasize it in performance? Does the meaning of the text suggest the kind of speed we might choose or whether we shall sing smoothly or *staccato*? These decisions and choices are crucial in performance and the act of composition. When children are asked to listen to music with words we might first look at these and develop some ideas about the kind of music we may hear. To take a very familiar example from the *Messiah*: what kind of music might we have for words like 'Hallelujah', 'King of Kings and Lord of Lords'? It might be quiet, gentle or tentative but is it likely? If a crowd of people are feeling something which makes them want to shout 'Hallelujah' are they going to shout at the same time or would we hear 'Hallelujah' at different times from different voices? In these ways we are preparing for a direct relationship with the chorus itself and the notation of the words has given a focus. How different this is from beginning with a potted history of oratorio or the life of Handel. We have tried to prepare for knowing *it*. Knowing *that* it is by Handel and any other information can, if we choose, follow later.

A similar strategy of exploration can be adopted when the words of songs are in a foreign language. Do we need to give the translation before people hear them? Or, might we not ask, 'What kind of words do you think they are, and what kind of things do you think the singer is singing about'?

For example, we have in mind a protest song sung by Mercedes Sosa from the Argentine (*Hermano, Dame tu Mano*). The words are in Spanish, of course. Before the first hearing we would ask whether there are changes during the song. We might discover that it has three distinct parts, each one a little firmer and more march-like than those before. The first section is sung as a smooth line and seems to be inviting us to consider something, or perhaps is telling a story. The second part is more determined, more insistent, more urgent and, at one point the music seems to dance in an impetuous way. The third section is quite simply a march, very determined indeed, sung with a hard voice and at the loudest level so far. We are dealing here with expressive qualities as perceived in the song as well as with its structure or form. The Spanish words may now illustrate our discoveries in translation. The first part is an invocation — 'Brother give me your hand, let's go together to find a little thing called freedom'. The more determined part in the middle asks us to 'look forward brother, the world waits for you without frontiers to hold up your hand and pull down the hand of the lord of the chains' (the tyrant). The march-like section section has the words:

> *'Forward with the march*
> *Forward with the drum*
> *Forward with the people in my song'.*

The notation of these words may now take us forward into further listening and performance — the chorus is easy enough to sing in Spanish. Every teacher will surely think of other examples near to hand where this strategy may be helpful. In particular, for example, we might think of those pupils preparing for a 16+ examination for whom it seems important to become familiar (among other things) with *Lieder*. Since the recordings we have are likely to be in German might we not leave aside for a while what we know of the translation and ask what the words *might* be about, where the tensions are, whether the song flows and is easy-going or changes dramatically. What is the piano doing? Of course we are not going to get a literal construction of what the text actually says but surely we are going to find some of the expressive elements in this way and to notice the repetitions and changes that generate the structure of the song.

In a similar way the notation of words on a blackboard may give us something to follow, the music can be mapped out by reference to these words, we are better able to discuss it and draw each other's attention to what we notice. Take as an example the beautiful song known to many teenagers at the time of writing — *Killing Me Softly With His Song* sung by Roberta Flack. The chorus is as follows:

> *Strumming my pain with his fingers*
> *Singing my life with his words*
> *Killing me softly with his song*
> *Killing me softly with his song*
> *Telling my whole life with his words*
> *Killing me softly with his song*

What do we make of the title? As we listen do we detect a special shape in the music? Is it possible to say anything about the differences between each pair of lines? The first two lines seem fairly square and straightforward but the middle pair seem to float upwards. Over the last two lines the music seems to gently spiral down to the last word. If we join in singing having noticed such things we shall surely sing more sensitively and meaningfully.

We might notice how these things are achieved. The last six lines only have one explicit first beat in the vocal line, all the others are hidden by syncopations. The floating feeling is partly conveyed in this way and partly through the slow descent over an octave by step, with few angular leaps. These musical shapes fuse into a long 9-bar phrase which, because it is long and irregular, gives a strong impression of freedom — a kind of musically controlled parachute jump. We might notice these things, but it is much more important to experience them than to talk about them or label them. Conversations about music *are* important, but the art of a good conversationalist lies in knowing when to listen.

One final instance of the use of words as notation involves starting with words. Working in pairs or groups, children might be asked to invent questions and answers. There might be urgent questions, careful questions, abrupt questions and submissive answers, assertive answers, reflective answers. What happens if we substitute music for words? What happens if the music becomes more heated and active if the questions and answers speed up, overlap and grow in loudness? Could we stop it by simmering down slowly or by breaking up into fragments? Listen to the first of *Five Pieces for Orchestra*, Schoenberg, Opus 16. It requires a lot of attention and is very concentrated, things happen quickly. But some of the characteristics of this work have already been approached. We hear a warm string sound, slightly urgent — a kind of question? The sounds of wind respond, hard and cold — a kind of answer? This happens three times, each time differently and the last answer is positively harsh. There is more movement, pressing in, growing louder. The music turns into a driving march, heavy and powerful, then breaks into fragments which become an echo of the march and it is all over. If we can agree on a rough verbal notation for this and list the key words — warm, cold, harsh, etc — we may have more purchase on the music next time round. It is helpful to begin to substitute symbols for words at this stage, thus moving closer towards the more usual concept of what a notation is (though words often serve us very well). These symbols can be devised and used to notate pupils' compositions and might help them to develop and refine their pieces. For example, the relative position in space may indicate higher or lower sounds while the symbol itself indicates loudness (size) duration (length) and manner of attack and release (shape).

GRAPHIC NOTATIONS
We must be sure at this stage that the notation does not become a visual pattern for its own sake. It is simply a tool to help us to follow, work with and recall music.

Sometimes building up a graphic score from what is heard, stage by stage, helps to sharpen awareness of texture and instrumental colour. Take this simple and beautiful Irish tune, *The Praties They Grow Small*.

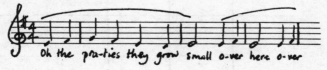

here, oh the pra-ties they grow small and we
dig them in the fall, And we eat them skins and
all, o- ver here, o- ver here.

As it stands the notation tells us a fair amount, mainly about
pitch and rhythm, though the use of words 'quite slow' gives
further important information. If however we listen to the
recording by Ian and Lorna Campbell we shall hear a texture in
which the vocal line is only one element. Building it up verse by
verse may eventually give us something like this. (Here again
though, we must be careful that the aural and written skills
involved do not so completely monopolise our attention so as
to displace the beauty of the tune and the pathetic and significant words.)

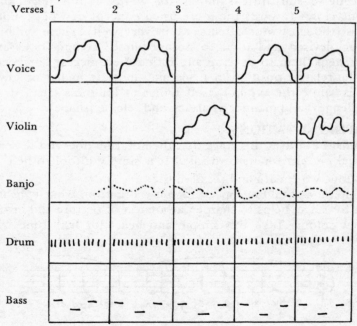

Once we have a score of this kind it is not only possible to follow music with it but also to take it as a starting place for new compositions. We could use any instruments or voices to invent a piece of music based on these shapes and textures. We may use the simple note row of *The Praties*

or take any series of pitches but conserving the shape and the rhythm, as in this pentatonic series

Alternatively, the composition need bear no resemblance at all to the original apart from the gentle arching shape and could sound very 'modern', perhaps without metre or melody in the traditional sense.

Sometimes staff notation has a remarkable similarity to certain expressive features of music. One well-known work, often played at concerts and in schools, can be directly approached through the 'look' of the notation which may tell us more than the conventional 'programme' with *The Hebrides Overture* by Mendelssohn. Here traditional notation is graphic in effect and could easily be represented in other ways.

The attentive 'eye' is impressed in a similar way to the listening 'ear', by a contrast between what is happening in the top stave and the bottom. The lower stave has more going on, it is busier, while the higher stave has fewer notes that sit on lines

or in space, gradually piling up one on top of the other. So the eye has an impression of movement and stillness presented *at the same time*. Are our pupils discovering this for themselves or being told about Mendelssohn feeling sea-sick or whatever? If they are searching the score then the ear is already being tuned to notice the held wind unisons and chords, and the movement at the lower pitch of violas and 'cellos. No wonder that this music reminds us to some extent of the contrast of the constantly moving sea and stationary rocks piled up, like the notes of those chords, on top of one another. It is possible to penetrate further into this work by indentifying the ways in which the movement and stillness develop. For example, before long the 'still' notes grow and diminish rapidly and quite frighteningly.

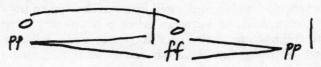

Later on these still sounds become attached to a fanfare.

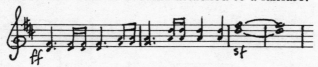

At the same time ghostly fragments of movement flicker around the orchestra. Anyone who is aware of these things is launched into this music in a way that makes the 'programme' seem rather tame and uneventful. The Overture is *full* of events.

Whether or not we want to play a recording of *The Hebrides* there are many ideas to be found there which deserve attention. For instance, we could initiate a project where the possibilities of 'busy versus still' are to be explored. In groups or pairs or as a whole class we could assemble busy and still sounds. What makes a sound 'still' anyway? Now the most striking busy and still sounds can be selected, related to one another in a composition and performed with the intention to communicate this or that *kind* of stillness and activity. There is after all a vast difference between the sharp craggy stillness of the *sf* here,

compared with the more ominous stillness of this *crescendo-diminuendo*.

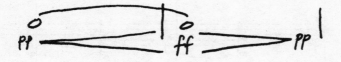

These last bits of notation have a look about them that strongly resembles the growth and diminution of sound. Traditional notation has very few of these directly analogous markings and at this point a group engaged in composition and performance of 'Busy-Still' pieces may need to generate a few more graphic symbols to handle, say, frantic busy-ness as opposed to mechanical busy-ness, or the stillness of sand dunes rather than the stillness of frozen trees. The only rules for inventing notation are that it must be easy to write or draw and it ought to be as suggestive as possible of the musical ideas it resembles.

A sample of notational vocabulary

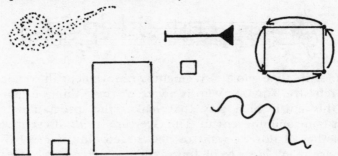

One instance of very still, almost static music, would be the third of Schoenberg's *Five Orchestral Pieces*. The problem for the listener here is the opposite of that encountered with *Premonitions*. The rate of change is very slow, though the movement is not very long. Yet if we really listen and focus our attention on the small changes they do, after a short while, become very significant. The notation used by the players looks something like this version of the first two bars.

It may help concentration to try to devise a notation for *listeners* and the first three bars might be represented something like this. (Remember though, listening comes first and the visual ideas really ought to come from the class.)

The only change is the slightly different instrumental colour

between the first and second half of each bar. But the next
three bars are more eventful.

To perceive these changes is to notice harmonic change of a
quite subtle order. The effect is strange. The music seems to be
squeezing gently this way and that and as it moves on it becomes more and more eventful with dabs of sound ♪♪ and specks
of sound. ♪♪♪ By this time the notation will have done its work
and the scale on which the musical events take place will be
grasped. Once this happens the barriers between us and the
work are lifted and it all makes sense, from the particular quality of stillness we first observed to the glittering, flashing
ideas that are deftly splashed into the texture later on. The
title, *Summer Morning by a Lake/Colours* might now be noticed, although Schoenberg was unhappy about using titles
and put them in really to please his publisher, who in turn
seemed to think that people could not enjoy the music unless
they were thinking about something else. Over 60 years later,
have we improved our own receptivity, let alone the awareness
of those whom we teach? Certainly the title makes sense once
we are inside the music and the attempt to devise a notation
may help. If not then it should be abandoned. If we really have
explored the compositional possibilities of stillness and busy-
ness then it seems far more likely that the music of Schoenberg
will get the attention it deserves, along with that of Mendelssohn,
whose music survives its popularity and appears as 'fresh as
paint' every time we really listen rather than merely label.

SPACE AND BALANCE

Concepts of space and balance are not easily depicted in traditional notation and special forms of graphic representation are
needed to embody such ideas as distance, direction, background
and foreground sounds and *sound-collage*. In a strange way the
music of Gabrieli's in sixteenth century Venice is very much at
home today in the world of stereo recording. We know that the
space in *St Mark's* church, Venice was used with good effect
to separate and distance choral or instrumental sound so that
elaborate and striking mixes, blends and contrasts could take
place. Take for instance part of a setting of the *Magnificat* by
Andrea Gabrieli. Here the three choirs answer one another at
a distance and distinctively in clusters of high, middling and low
voices.

Very different in some ways, but still dependent on a sense
of space, distance and colour contrasts, is *Grüppen* by Stockhausen, or to a more limited extent, the more approachable
Kontakte. It is the drier percussion sounds that seem to 'travel'
best across the speakers of stereo equipment. These are explored
in fascinating spacial ways in Varèse's *Intégrales*. What strikes
us first about this music? Firstly and often there is a kind of
trumpet call played on the clarinet and later on trumpet and
transformed on the oboe. But around these calls are dabs,
spots, flurries and splashes of sound on percussion that appear
to come from each side and (an illusion) from behind or in
front of each other. It is worth separating the speakers a little
further than usual if possible to amplify this effect. The expressive character is organised in fairly separate and clear passages.
After the trumpet has 'spoken' a 'snarling' brass chord trans-
forms the music into a slower, heavier progression with cymbals
and low trombone sounds against higher trombone calls. Then a
whistle of woodwind pushes the music into a strange and brief

kind of march. But all the time our ears are kept alert by the colour, balance and direction of the sounds, always changing and on the move in space.

How might we prepare other people, our classes, to notice and respond to these elements? One possibility is to use an ordinary portable cassette recorder. Establish four quite different groups of sounds, perhaps wood, metal, vocal humming and strings. Let each group develop a fairly steady pattern in its own corner of the room. Then let someone travel to and from the groups with the mobile recorder (which is an ear with a memory). Now we listen. If each group has been visited properly we shall hear the balance shift. As one comes into the foreground so others recede into the distance. Can we make a musical composition in this way and decide beforehand where the mechanical 'ear' will go and in what sequence? What would happen if we used one group as a repeated idea and used the others as contrasts? The notation for this might look something like a map of a journey.

Start and stop

To play this to another group would make an interesting aural exercise. Can they follow and 'notate' where the microphone goes?

A slightly more sophisticated version is to use stereo recording techniques and to place the players relative to one microphone or the other. We are now drawing closer to the recording studio setting and can control the levels and balance either by playing quietly or loudly or by adjusting the levels on the tape-recorder. These techniques and the developing listening skills must, of course, become servants of musical ideas. By now there may be several ideas emerging, but if not we could think about taking an existing composition and perform it with different levels of recording, deciding which sounds the most effective, or we could develop the ideas of space and balance along with contrasting groupings into more substantial compositions. Music already mentioned by Gabrieli, Varèse and Stockhausen will certainly begin to make sense if this kind of project is generated.

STAFF NOTATION

Staff notation has been a contentious issue for a long time. Many teachers have regarded it as basic to music and want 'notation' to be learned by children at school. But what do we mean by 'learning notation'? What can a person *do* when he or she has 'learned notation'? This is the crucial question and it often proves very difficult to obtain a clear answer. There are obviously different levels of achievement and no one has 'learned' staff notation to 100 per cent. For instance, who could mentally hear in every detail and with every nuance of instrumental colour a work such as Bartok's *Bluebeard's Castle*, especially if the work had *never* been heard in performance. To be able to do this would be a remarkable instance of someone who had 'learned' notation. Most of us function at various other levels. We might be able to 'hear' any Haydn symphony in our heads from the score and perhaps control the balance of parts so as, for example, to emphasise the horns or oboes here and there. Or we might be able to sing at sight the tenor part in the chorus of Brahms' *Requiem*. Or we might be able to pick out a tune on the piano with one finger because we know the names of the notes on paper and the keys on the instruments. Or we may be able to follow a printed copy while listening. So when we say that pupils should learn notation we ought to specify *what they will be able to do*.

Unfortunately not everyone thinks in this way and as a result we have just seen a generation of children pass through our schools who can label the parts of notation — this is a crotchet, a trill, an Eb — but cannot use them. That is to say, they could not take a written tune away and learn to play it without a lot of help, let alone sing a simple melody at sight. The *theory of notation* is what is often taught, not the ability to read or write music down while knowing how it sounds.

Because of this the new convention is to denegrate staff notation and any systematic attempts to teach people how to use it, such as Sol-fa or graded sight-singing schemes. We do not wish to enter into this contention here but would merely point out that some facility with notation can be helpful not only when composing and performing but also when in audience to music. Whether the necessary skills are best acquired unconsciously by standing 'next to Nellie' in a choir or whether a more systematic approach is needed is a matter of judgement. All we can say is that some people stand next to Nellie for a long time but still can never be depended on as music

readers. We are not concerned so much here with the instrumen-
talist who learns to use notation, instrument in hand, and in an
ensemble but with the majority of young people at school. It
does seem a pity that a class who enjoy singing should not also
enjoy reading music at an appropriate level of difficulty, whether
the notation be the Curwen hand-signs in the first instance or a
one or two line stave. To take one other instance, in many
schools it would be perfectly possible to prepare the ground
in such a way that a small group could find a place to work
and, independently of the teacher, develop an instrumental
performance from printed parts or written-out rhythm *ostinati*.
At least these people would leave school with an idea of how
staff notation 'works'.

Such competences depend to a large extent on building up
sets of skills incrementally over a period of time and the danger
here is that the enterprise turns into an arid and dull series of
exercises. 'Barking at print' is not enough. Knowing how to
read something must move into knowing the 'it' of performance, while knowing how to write something ought to be closely
linked with composition. The ability to follow notation can
only be developed and used in audience to music and may at
times be the first contact in a more sustained encounter.

A good example of this integration of notational skills with
listening can be found in *Approach to Music*, Book 1, by Renouf
and Smith (OUP). The authors have been developing ways of
encouraging sight-singing, instrumental playing and composition
using just five notes:

They then show five notes strung together in quick runs.

A Little Joke by Dmitri Kabalevsky is built from such flourishes
against the contrast of *staccato* quavers,

Subsequent listening and looking reveals that in the middle of the piece the runs are reversed:

We could go further and take the idea of runs or (easier) *glissandi* on xylophones set against dry, hard pairs of sounds, perhaps unpitched, as a basis for a class or group composition. We might also notice the stirring effect of the upward flourishes when repeated grandly by trumpets as they are at the start of Monteverdi's *Orfeo*. Notice the stately way in which the tune descends. Here are more ideas for compositions where going up a series of notes is sharply contrasted with the manner of coming down, perhaps alternatively as Monteverdi does or perhaps keeping one of them for a middle section.

Many teachers feel that it is possible and valuable to develop at least the reading of common rhythm patterns. In 2/4 time these might be as follows.

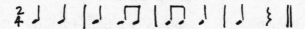

The acquisition of reading skills here depends on the 'three R's' of Recording (hearing often and associating what is heard with what is seen), Recognising (identifying the patterns in any order), and finally Reading (playing them in any order, at different speeds and levels of loudness). This does not have to be a chore and can be linked with the invention of patterns in question and answer fashion and the building up of longer compositions based on *ostinati*. The crucial thing is to be sure that there is a sense of structure and some expressive character. Nothing is worse than brutal hand-clapping in a mechanical way. For example, let us assume that the four patterns above have been mastered, that is to say can be recognised and read either within a 2/4 or 4/4 organisation. The following piece might be read, rehearsed and performed. It is *gentle* and steady and the top part may be finger-clicking or Indian Bells or may be on pitched instruments confined to the first three notes of a minor scale played up and down in steps. The effect can be very beautiful, relaxed and slightly sad.

Now we can follow this while listening to the theme of the *Enigma Variations* by Elgar. Here we meet the same kind of feeling, certainly the same rhythms, but instead of the cymbal the 'cellos and basses move from note to note. The texture is fairly rich compared with ours. There is also a short span of different material in the middle followed by what we already know. What would happen if we took up the moving bass line idea and played our three notes pattern, two notes to a bar against the tune we might have had before?

(continued overleaf)

This is safe enough but what would happen if different groups took different rows of notes (see Chapter Four) and composed a tune and stepping bass-lines using these rhythms? Or what would happen if we left out the crotchet rest and turned the rhythm into 3/4 time at a fast speed and loud?

The fourth Variation of the *Enigma* does just this. Or what would happen if we played the 3/4 version slowly and smoothly? Variation nine, *Nimrod*, is like that.

Once again we ought to notice that 'knowing about' is secondary to knowing the music directly and that the skills involved in knowing *how*, how to read notation, handle the instruments and so on, is always the servant of knowing *this* piece, *this* musical idea, *this* composition. Notation can easily side-track us, but if we use it wisely and with imagination there is greater potential for purposeful and musical activity.

Even the simplest rhythmic devices can flower into music of very different kinds. The *Allegretto* of the *Seventh Symphony* by Beethoven is built on the most basic pattern.

Janáček, in his *Sinfonietta* employs similar patterns with a totally different effect brought about by a strident use of brass.

The important thing is to discover the differences, structural and expressive, that can be made and found with the same scraps of notational skill. Heaven forbid that lively music should be reduced in the minds of our pupils to inert crotchets and quavers or to meaningless (even if pretty) graphic devices. In the beginning was the musical idea worked out in sound and at the end this is what remains, the irreducible experience of music as sound.

6
Context and Perspective

So far, in this book, we have stressed the necessity to attend to the specific art object, the promotion of active involvement with a *particular* piece of music, delving into its structural and expressive character. Our aim has been, and still is, to encourage our pupils to know 'what's what' in music and to foster a deep knowledge and familiarity with the music itself — to know 'it' and, we would hope, to find this way of knowing of value.

At this point it seems important to think a little more clearly about how these isolated encounters begin to connect, start to cluster, make some sort of pattern. In other words, how does the individual begin to knit these experiences together into an interlocking framework? In chapter two we examined first Bach's *Polonaise in G minor* in sufficient depth to tease out those expressive and structural qualities which led us further and further inside the music. It was, in fact, only at the end of this deep probing that we began to consider the supportive facts and information about the piece eg 'What is a polonaise (where does it originate, how does it relate to our ideas of dance in general)? Who composed *this* polonaise (his name, place in time, country, the information which builds a composite picture of Bach's achievements in the pattern of events)? Thus we attempt to put the particular into a context, rather like framing a picture. We begin to seek a social and cultural frame of reference.

KNOWLEDGE OF CONTEXT
It is particularly interesting to note the current trend for compilation record albums on which a seamless flow of 'clips' from the classics, or the pop charts is produced, backed by a regular, pulsating, four-square 'beat'. One could admit that an

elementary contextual knowledge is required to recognise and differentiate a 'Sheena Easton' from a 'Beatles' number. On the one hand the music can be listened to, or absorbed, as a new genre in its own right — a continuous, arranged piece of music. On the other we may play a kind of 'Spot the Tune' game rather like the television quiz programme 'Face the Music'. As teachers we may well be disturbed by the way in which the distinguishing characteristics and unique quality of each song have been diluted into a bland, international (or possibly 'anti-national) Muzak. This example of a current fashion has been described as it appears to run counter to the idea of individuality, personality or the 'integrity of the particular' which has been the theme of this book. In the face of music churned out 'by the yard' as it were, it is evident that the music teacher's business is more than ever concerned with separating out what has become so muddled; a point which will be returned to later.

In contributing to a contextual picture we can view human achievements in terms of individuals, groups and societies. We view them historically or vertically moving back and forward through time, in the process demonstrating *development*, *change*, *fashion*, *reaction*. Our knowledge of context also requires a *lateral* dimension to show how a musical work and its maker is placed in relation to other musical forms, styles and categories across the diverse range of the whole musical spectrum. A broader social and cultural perspective is obviously gained by a pupil's increasing general knowledge and learning experiences in, for example, allied arts, history, geography, literature. Nor is all culture homogeneous. There are conflicting strands and movements, reactionaries and radicals in every age. A contextual knowledge is fed by many considerations and growing experience in technical 'know-how', (eg the recognition of a constantly flattened leading note placing a piece in pre-Renaissance times before the ascendancy of instrumental music). And then there is the biographical perspective which helps us to know something of a composer's intentions, the circumstances in which he worked and the motivating forces which tended to shape his development.

NOTION OF A CATEGORY
These then are some of the perspectives which begin to intertwine, giving a feeling of context and development. At this point, let us explore some potential avenues of approach which may contribute to this process of mapping out the musical

terrain. For the purpose of the exercise we will consider music under four obvious headings: *type*; *function*; *place*; and *time*. At the same time it must be stressed that these are only instances. They are neither comprehensive nor exclusive. We are not endeavouring to map out the whole field of interrelated musics. That would take a book or series of books. The aim here is simply to demonstrate potential ways in which sensitivity to context can be assisted and reinforced by developing some notion of a category.

TYPE

What if we were to take as a theme the idea of 'folksong'. We could begin with a simple example like the following, probing it for those expressive and structural characteristics which might provide the answer to: 'What type of song is this?'

Green Gravel

We would expect to build up a composite picture with our pupils along the following lines:

Rhythmically: simple, swaying, almost clock-like, constantly returning to a point of rest;

Melodically: simple, straightforward, limited to a range of five notes (D to A first half, G to D second half): again, constantly returning to base or home note;

Structure: fairly homogeneous, a four bar phrase repeated exactly; in the second half the same phrase is sung at a higher level (transposed up a fourth).

The overall sing-song quality would be recognised instantly for what it is, a children's traditional song, – in this case a singing game which would be reinforced by the addition of the words:

> *Green gravel, green gravel,*
> *The grass is so green;*
> *The fairest young damsel*
> *That ever was seen.*
> *O Mary, O Mary,*
> *Your true love is dead,*
> *He sends you this letter,*
> *For to turn round your head.*

But we have, in fact, taken our children deeper into the music to determine those characteristics which appear in a traditional children's song. We can then check these out against another model to see if the characteristics are constant:

Rhythmically: simple, moves along yet often comes to rest, interesting short-long metre at the beginning;

Melodically: mainly adheres to range of five notes with the exception of moving down to low E and D. It does not stray very far and there is frequent repetition of ♩♩♩ 𝄽 with an interesting melodic uncertainty by ending on A rather than on G, apart from final phrase;   *216464*

Structure: fairly unified, a basic idea is repeated and the second half of the song is a variation of the first.

This song shares so many similarities with our first example that we can categorise this as another children's song, although the information from both the music and the words may not, in themselves be sufficient to inform us that this is a Jamaican children's song.

But this time here is another simple yet significantly different song type:

Rhythmically: rather free-flowing, the notation suggests freedom and there are constant changes of time, with quite long rests between phrases;

Melodically: covers a range of seven notes with ornamentation, glissandi, a constant rise and fall, ebb and flow. We would notice the decoration of the second phrase when it re-appears at the end;

Structure: unified — an opening and answering phrase which are repeated in varied form.

If we asked who might be singing this, it is fairly safe to say a solo singer rather than a group. The simplicity of the style, as with the children's songs denotes that it is a folk song. The fact that in its rise and fall, ebb and flow, it is compressed with what Deryck Cooke in *The Language of Music* (1959) describes as '*emotion in musical form*' presents us with a prime example of the solo folk song. Here we have a leisurely flow, time for taking breath, the opportunity to decorate vocally and to bend the time, treating the song in a wholly individual manner. Some of these examples could be used as models for pupils' compositions eg compose a children's song using only five notes or compose a solo song which is free flowing and ornamented. We could return to the folk songs quoted in earlier chapters and use these as models. There was the Jewish song '*Shalom Chaverin*' (Chapter One, p.12) with its antiphonal feeling, simple structure and the almost organic way in which the melody grew and retracted. Akin to this was the Irish tune '*The Praties they grow small*' (Chapter Five) which rose and fell from a germ-like unit of four notes.

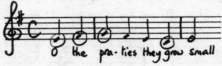

and was unified by the repeated phrase

In chapter three there was the American *Five Hundred Miles*, rhythmically unified in range (pentatonic), repetitious in terms of words, rhythm and melodic shape. And then there was the heavier and robust *Padstow Song* with a strong rhythmic drive, melodically more wide-ranging, yet still a simple, unified song.

At some stage, we would hope that the notion of folk-song would be absorbed into our pupils' experience. With guidance they could be helped to articulate what appear to be the distinguishing characteristics of folk song:

— a form of music which has grown up among the mass of the population of any race;
— at one time transmitted orally;
— needs no accompaniment;
— always verse repeating;
— often not written in modern scale but in old modes;
— usually of limited vocal range;
— often antiphonal in nature, either by alternating solo and

chorus phrases, or by verse with follow-up chorus.

We might delve more deeply into the historical development of folk-song. A.L. Lloyd's *Folk Song in England* provides a rich source of information from the communal song of clan society. to the individual or 'I' song of post-feudal times, both fused in the folk song of industrial societies. Here songs of communal concern (strike songs, disaster songs) combine both personal elements with feelings of class solidarity. And we might encourage our pupils to be collectors themselves, perhaps discovering current playground songs and chants or re-discovering songs from elderly relatives. We have quoted only a handful of examples but sufficient, we hope, to stimulate interest in the idea of folk-song as an example of 'type'.

FUNCTION

It follows on from here that much of the music described under the category 'type' has a clearly defined functional reason for its existence. In fact, we tend to forget that it is only in comparatively recent times that music has come to be regarded as a highly personal art form. The function of music in earlier civilisations and, as we often see today, was closely tied up with ceremony and ritual.

Children's game songs such as *Old Roger is Dead* are thought to be expressive ways of playing out the experience of bereavement and the ritual of burials. Seasonal songs such as the *Padstow Song* represent an annual ritualised custom. If these are thought to be aspects of play, there are also work songs such as sea-shanties, cowboy and drover songs. There is a wealth of music written for worship, the theatre, social and seasonal customs, work and play. This vast heritage stretches back into time from the mingling of the pagan and the Christian:

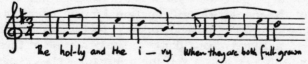

The hol-ly and the i — vy   When they are both full-grown

to the present day football chant:

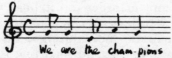

We are the cham-pions

from the dance-hymn of the early nineteenth century Shakers, a sect which settled in the USA for whom dancing was an integral part of their worship:

'Tis the gift to be sim-ple,'tis the gift to be free, 'Tis the
gift to come down where we ought to be, And when we find our-selves in the
place just right,'twill be in the val-ley of love and de-light.

to the *Promenade* dance theme from the musical of the same name.

One could prepare a list or a chart which would give some glimpse of the many fields of functional music including hymn, carol, mass, oratorio, musical, opera, processional music, ceremonial and military music, dance music. Any one of these categories could be taken as a starting point for a class assignment, exploring in depth the characteristics of particular musical examples of the genre in order to establish what makes it apt for its function eg what musical characteristics of the *Hallelujah Chorus* give it its majestic and exulting nature? Why does Mendelssohn's *Wedding March* sound so fitting for a bride to walk down the aisle to meet her groom? Compose a processional piece which is slow, stately and majestic or make up a dance tune of a celebratory nature. Write a song to accompany various work actions or a series of 'keep-fit' exercises. In view of what has been said about the function of music in earlier civilisations it is helpful to remind ourselves that today the mass media bring us a vast quantity of *functional* music. One could say that this is an up-dated twentieth century form of *ritual* music, music for sleeping, eating, shopping, etc. The problems and possibilities which the mass media pose for music teachers are treated in more detail in Dorothy Taylor's *Music Now* (1979) but it seems appropriate at this point to probe further into this aspect of functional music as it is an important issue affecting our work and our daily lives.

Inevitably we are surrounded today by a sheer quantity of music which encompasses: the spectrum from good, to bad, to indifferent; every conceivable style; diverse national to international sources. Packaged music accompanies us from supermarket to hotel lift. As 'convenience' music it is often as bland and insubstantial as sliced bread. Yet, it is difficult to understand how we absorb, and are affected by, its trivialities, its superficiality and its often ephemeral nature.

As teachers, aware of our responsibilities in educating the young, we recognise that the mass media conditions, manipulates and ensures a certain standardisation of the music market and of our musical expectations and responses. At the same time as these experiences are being absorbed our pupils are *learning*. And this learning process goes on with and without the help of the school. It must be remembered that much is being learnt sub-consciously, without any formal teaching at all. Inevitably part of our job as educators is to be aware of those social and commercial forces which help to shape our learning, affect our conceptions and expectations and, wherever possible, seek to relate what we do in the classroom to the wide context in which we all operate. It is also evident that the technological developments which first brought the gramophone into every household have accelerated during the last thirty years to provide a media resource bank of considerable size and potential. There is unparalleled accessibility to music in all its *quality* as well as quantity. Looking now at the positive aspects of this revolution, the music teacher has access to the hardware which makes the recording of music in the classroom possible and the means by which she can ensure extensive listening to music. The widening of these possibilities does enable more people to share in a broader base of musical experiences. Through this corporate knowledge, the imaginative educator is able to penetrate, draw attention to the particular, the distinctive and the unusual. Through *purposeful* activities, designed to encourage *active listening* rather than *passive hearing*, we may at least aim to develop discriminative powers in our pupils. Thus they may become aware of the way in which music serves particular functions and may be helped to disentangle the threads with some attempt at objectivity.

As television and film are so powerful a medium in our lives, we will focus on those aspects which offer most potential to music teachers. It is interesting to observe how, over the last few years, the quality of music associated with television advertising, has improved by leaps and bounds. Whilst cigarette manufacturers still tend to cling to clichés and stereotypes of 'pastoral' or 'mountain-fresh' musical images, the promotion of Italian cars is often accompanied by the music of Rossini and Verdi. Again, Orff's *Carmina Burana* has proved to be a popular accompaniment to products ranging from toiletries to various brands of tyres.

More subtle, perhaps, are the associational ideas which stem from the theme music to films or serials. How many children have been exposed to Prokofiev's *Classical Symphony*, through its use as theme music to a serialised story: *The Flaxton Boys*? For many viewers the mere thought of Daphne du Maurier's *Rebecca* evokes the first bars of Debussy's Prelude — *Des Pas sur la Neige* (Footprints in the Snow).

An evening's viewing could be not only entertaining but productive if we were to tape-record several examples of advertising jingles and theme music. However, the purpose here is not to advocate tape-recording merely to use in a form of quiz which effectively tests which of our pupils are the most avid television viewers. (This, as critics of the 'mastermind' context would avow, might merely prove to be a test of memory.) Instead, these tape-recordings could be used as a resource bank of extracts to be analysed for their expressive and structural qualities and then judged for their appropriateness to the function intended by the advertiser.

As educators there is much we could do to encourage our pupils to reflect on media music and our perceptions of it. Particularly is this so when it is understandably difficult for any one of us to view it objectively. How often do we ask ourselves to what extent are we conditioned by media music and the form of association through repetition which links a product with visual and aural images, however inappropriate they may be. We are all very familiar with 'programme' music where music has been inspired by a theme, an idea, a poem, quotation, legend, or composed specifically for a play, or film such as *I Claudius*. And then there is what one might term music 'matching', where a composition is chosen according to its suitability for setting an atmosphere, giving the character of what one is to see on the screen. A typical example here has already been mentioned — *Des Pas sur la Neige* by Debussy — the theme for *Rebecca*:

Des Pas sur la Neige seems to encapsulate the prevailing sadness of the story, a mysterious and slowly evolving tale of a young wife who is living in the constant shadow of her husband's first wife and her inexplicable, mysterious death. The theme music seems perfectly matched. What is it about this prelude that gives it such a plaintive character?
— is it the rising, rather hesitant seconds in the left hand, which appear constantly through the piece and appear to be the germ from which everything else grows?
— is it the melodic line, part of which is quoted above?

At the same time we should be asking ourselves:

— to what extent have we been predisposed or conditioned by the composer's expressive markings ie *triste et lent*; *expressif et douloureux*; and, *'ce rhythme doit avoir la valeur sonore d'un fond de paysage triste et glacé* (the sound of this figure should convey the depths of a black and frozen landscape)?

Another recent television serial *We the Accused* had for its theme and incidental music, specifically composed and equally mind-haunting music:

Again one might ask to what extent is this ethereal, wistful, sadness a result of association of images — aural, visual and dramatic, or, is this particular expressive quality bound up with the essential character of the music (the rise and fall of the line, the minor key, the arrangement for high echoing female voice, piano, and cimbalon)?

This is obviously a controversial and challenging field for study, yet an important one, for us to explore with our pupils. In their book *Teaching as a Subversive Activity* Postman and Weingartner describe 'label-libel' as the human ability to pigeonhole an idea, an activity or a process which once labelled can be conveniently disposed of without further thought. This is not to deny that music has undeniable associations in the mind of the listener. In the particular cases which we have described, however, it may well be the matching or using of one piece of music to tie it to another art form or idea which, for good or ill, often 'label-libels'. For those who experience it, the association may be sufficient to trap together the two artefacts permanently. This is not a recent phenomenon, for pianists in the 'silent' movie days inevitably established permanent associations for music and film in much the same way.

So we are suggesting that we recognise the function and explore as objectively as we can the range of 'media music' to which we are exposed. Recently there was a re-showing on television of the film *Zapata* (starring Yul Brynner) an example of the familiar genre of cowboy films set in Mexico. This film is accompanied by incidental music of wide-ranging colour and effectiveness, which can be captured on tape and replayed without the need for visual images. From the haunting, whistled tune:

which constantly recurs, to the quick utterances of suspense heard in the piano' writing and the trombones ♩♩ to the movement of horses and riders with their ♫♫♪ rhythmic figure, there is ample material here for classroom work to focus on questions such as:

1   for what kind of film has this particular music been chosen or composed — pick out the clues from focussing on the qualities of melody, rhythm, harmony, instrumentation, timbre, texture, dynamics, tempi, etc?

2   is the choice in every way appropriate — do you have better suggestions? Are there other rhythmic figures which might convey galloping, cantering, trotting for example?

Musical activities which could follow on from this might include the composing of music for an advertisement or a play (perhaps for one being performed in class). Alternatively, short pieces could be worked out for different atmospheric effects eg ghostly, haunting, eerie and dark for a mystery film; lively, clear, quick-moving for a comedy; music for a space journey or a hang-gliding demonstration, or differing qualities of human and animal movement. A filmed sequence could be shown after which pupils work in groups to compose incidental music for it.

In sum, none of us is immune to the influences of the mass media. At the very least we could alert our pupils to the functional aspect of the music which surrounds us and explore with them the associations which have been described. By encouraging each other to disentangle some of these connections, we might hope to counterbalance the simplistic or stereotyped, and encourage a sense of context and perspective.

PLACE

Thirdly we might search for those distinguishing characters which determine a piece of music's cultural origin or national identity. Again, for ease of accessibility we might start by selecting a sample of folk songs from our resources. Compare, for example, *Gypsy Davey*:

with *A la Claire Fontaine*

The first appears to be a sturdy, square-cut $\frac{2}{4}$ time, unequivo-cal moving to a different note whenever transferring from weak to strong. On the other hand, the latter, although in $\frac{2}{4}$ time, seems more pointed. more lilting. There is a feeling of 'holding back' before leaning into the strong accent. Compare the first four notes of *Gypsy Davy* with *A la Claire Fontaine*:

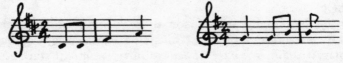

We notice the French song, unlike the English, does *not* change pitch from weak to strong. Does this tend to give it a more delicate lilting quality? Looking at the phrase lengths in the English song they are four bars long, in the French — two. Is this on account of the greater precision of the French language and should we be asking ourselves if the French, in fact, are able to say what they want to convey in less space than the English? Does this impose on the music shorter, recurring rhythmic units?

Here is another example, this time a Hungarian folk song:

English translation:

Through my window falls the moonlight
Shining from the sky above.
Through my window falls the moonlight
Shining from the sky above.
One I cherished, loved him only
Yet he left me, left me lonely,
He it was who stole my treasure,
Broke my heart, deserted me.

where we hear and see a mixture of curving, plaintive melody and sharp, spicy rhythmic punch. With our knowledge of the music of Kodály and Bartók, we would recognise the typical ♪♩.rhythm which gives Hungarian music its ethnic flavour. In pursuing our research further into the workings of the Hungarian language we would discover that Hungarian music tends not to have an anacrusis ♪♩imply because the language has no anacrusis and that this ♪♩. is an integral rhythm resulting from the fact that Hungarian words take a heavy stress on the first syllable eg *Bartók* and *Kodály* (pronounced *Ko*-dye).

We could similarly explore songs from the Caribbean eg the syncopated quality of *Wood Slave and Rice*

from Scotland, Ireland (see Chapter Five *Oh the Praties*) to map out their flavour and individual characteristics, looking further for the linguistic, cultural, social and historical clues which make the music what it is.

We have taken as models a sample of folk songs. Yet some of the most easily approachable and available music to explore could well be Spanish music, including not only music by Spanish composers but also the Frenchmen Bizet and Ravel for whom Spain, its atmosphere and its dances, held a special fascination.

Let us begin with the slow movement from Rodrigo's *Guitar Concerto de Aranjuez* with its melancholic grandeur, punctuated by the decoration of significant notes.

This could be compared with the Gypsies Chorus from Bizet's *Carmen* both by singing it and listening to it on record.

Again, despite the differing tempi and expressive intent of these two extracts, there is a similar feeling of rhythmic intensity. We would ask ourselves again, does this show the close relationship of the music with the Spanish language, with the nature of Spanish dance? We notice, in the second extract, the same characteristic decorative element. Appreciating the immense popularity of the guitar in Spain and the playing technique involved, it appears that in general Spanish vocal, orchestral and piano' music is inspired by the guitar. In fact it is as if the composer is attempting to convey the sound and soul of the guitar through a different medium. Contributing to this is the rhythmic stamping, clicking of the singers and dancers and the use of instruments such as castanets and tambourines. Many of our pupils will have some familiarity with the country, albeit with the commercialised areas of Majorca and the Costa Brava. Yet the opportunities they will have experienced to glimpse the rhythmic, driving and impassioned nature of the flamenco may give them insight and background into this particular area of musical experience.

Albeniz' *Prelude* from *Cantos de Espana* was one of our musical models in Chapter Four. Similarly the Rodrigo slow movement theme could be taken as a model of a theme which is presented first by one instrumental tone colour and then by another in a decorated version. Group compositions could evolve from this idea, giving opportunities to find out by trial and error the many ways in which a melody can be ornamented and varied. For example, the question could be raised — how many different ways could we decorate a note?

Cross reference would be helpful here to pieces such as *Malaguena*, another piece of Albeniz where the triplet decoration gives a more leisurely, lilting feeling to the melodic line:

and to de Falla's *Dance of Terror*, with the insistent snapping of a fast repetition of the principal note:

As we have seen, examples are easily found for exploration and comparison. By acute aural observation, by providing opportunities to use these examples as models for compositions, the essential characteristics of music from differing cultures and geographical sources can be more easily absorbed into each pupil's experience.

TIME
And finally we come to the 'time' element — the sense of historical perspective. Through all our music teaching we would hope to be inculcating a gradual feeling for style and period. However it would be in the upper years of school, the fifth and sixth in particular, where we would hope to see the most appre-

ciation and feeling for this kind of distinction. *Also*, by this stage, our pupils are able to draw on their expanding general knowledge and understanding to help form a reliable musical, historical and cultural framework.

There are many excellent reference books available for mapping out the terrain of musical history in which are charted the essential differences between the baroque, the classical, romanticism and serialism. However, with our guiding principle of moving straight to the music, let us with our pupils look for particular instances to illuminate those shifts which take place between one period and another.

We could turn to the first few bars of four piano sonatas to observe the changes which took place between the Classical period and the Romantic. The first composed in the mid-eighteenth century is a *Sonata in Eb major* by Haydn:

What do we notice about the music? We would be likely to comment on its general feeling of *balance* and *proportion*, a two-bar unit of bubbly fragments balanced by a singing legato descending line. The texture is crystal clear, mostly three part writing, with sufficient rests to give a feeling of lightness and air. We might say that it was *graceful* and *delicate*.

We could next compare this with an early sonata by Beethoven *Opus 2 No. 1 in F minor*, composed in 1795 and dedicated to his former teacher Haydn:

Again we would notice a general feeling of *symmetry*, an elegance and refinement. This time we hear a development of the opening two bar phrase, leading to a climatic spread *ff* chord in bar 7 and, if we were to go further, a dramatic pause in bar 8. The texture is again clear, with plenty of air but less so than in Haydn, for here there are three and four part chords in the bass part. We are left, then, with a feeling that although this extract is like the Haydn in spirit, there are already hints of a more *dramatic* or *emotional* character to the music.

We move on now to a sonata which Beethoven composed nine years later, *the Waldstein* Opus 53. Here we notice a clear and distinctive change:

There is no anacrusis. We go straight into the music (this time an allegro *con brio*) — low reiterated chords out of which a short melody line emerges. It is mysterious, dramatic, exploring the low sonority of the piano. There is much less air in the texture. Unlike the previous example, there is no clear melodic line. Instant modulation takes place as the first four bars are repeated a tone lower, again reinforcing the mysterious quality by moving to a darker key.

From this we go to Beethoven's last sonata *Opus 111 in C minor* written in 1822 just five years before his death.

In comparison with the previous examples, this opening introductory passage which precedes the tumultuous '*allegro con brio ed appassionata*' is an explosion of sforzando chords, strong, dramatic, full of suspense, rhythmically energetic. The texture is predominantly thick and dark, punctuated by dynamic contrasts and brilliant arpeggiation.

By establishing a reference point in Haydn's work and then comparing three extracts from a composer's work (one considered to be a bridge between the Classical and Romantic periods) our pupils are beginning to appreciate the changes which took place in the space of *one* man's lifetime. In these extracts we perceive the expressive and structural characteristics which mark the emphasis on beauty and proportion in the Classical period and on expression of emotion in the Romantic.

The *Waldstein Sonata* opening in particular shows a sonority which was to epitomise the compositions of late Romantic pianists — composers such as Chopin, Liszt and Rachmaninoff. Here are the opening bars of Chopin's *Study no. 1 in A♭* (*Twelve Studies*, Opus 25) known as *the Shepherd Boy*:

One is conscious of sheer warmth of sound, a rich sonority, achieved by the way in which the single chord of A♭ has been spread out or arpeggiated. The top note of the chord resonates to produce a singing line. In the third study of Chopin's Opus 10, there is also a singing melodic line which is often remembered in its arrangement as a popular song — *How Still is the Night*. Again there is a richness of texture, a deep bass and ex-

tensive range. These studies are no mere exercises but works
of art in their own right. Naturally, *the Shepherd Boy* also
gives the performer an opportunity to display his technical
wizardry as is the case with Rachmaninoff's *Preludes* and
Liszt's *La Campanella*. Our pupils would remark on their
seeming difficulty. Again, the use of descriptive titles, as with
so much of the music of the Romantic period, suggests that
musical ideas have been stimulated by poetry or influenced
by the other arts. Now would be the appropriate time to learn
that, in the piano music of the period, of which there is an
abundance, virtuosity was a key element; that the piano under-
went technical developments (the extension of its range, for
example) and that a new way of playing went hand in hand
with these developments to result in a more sonorous sound,
sung melodic lines, rich multi-coloured chords and varied arpeggiation.

By again taking specific examples orchestral, chamber and
vocal music could be compared in similar fashion, concentrating
on the particular characteristics which distinguish say Mozart's
Symphony No. 41 from Berlioz' *Harold in Italy*, or Mozart's
Requiem with that of Brahms'.

Having made the initial discoveries for themselves, now
would be the time to turn to the information so readily available for affirmation, elaboration and detail. Building on what
has been learned by first hand observation they would then read
that the Romantic composer stressed poetry rather than pattern, expressed individuality, was inspired by literary themes
and often came from a literary background. But, and it should
be stressed, it is of little value to *read* about the 'loosening of
the tonal system', 'innovatory harmony', 'chromaticism' and
'rubato' unless such facts have made their own impact through
first hand experience as listeners, performers and composers.

7
Towards a Music Curriculum

So far we have been considering the generation of music-based activities with discovery as a main principle. Whatever the activity or piece of music, we have been looking for the development of a rich appreciation through the three activities of *composing*, *performance* and being *in audience*. It should be emphasised again that these activities are samples only and not an exclusive collection of materials. We have been more concerned to establish principles of procedure — the teacher as discoverer and the pupil as discoverer — rather than provide a course to be slavishly followed or, as is more usual, to be picked at in a piecemeal way. We have tried to show how particular skills in music and knowledge about music should be subservient to composition, audition and performance. It is also apparent that this way of working involves a considerable amount of discussion, trying out, rehearsing, replaying and remaking. There is much less room for telling about, copying down, or acquiring aural and dextrous skills disassociated from music itself. Working in this way helps us to develop a sense of musical purpose.

THE INEVITABILITY OF A CURRICULUM
We also need to acquire a general sense of direction as well as developing purposeful activities in the short term. The period of compulsory schooling lasts for 11 years at present and this places a professional responsibility on us to make certain that the time is put to good use, not wasted by aimless repetition or preoccupation with trivial things; not an aimless part of life, tolerable only because of evenings, weekends, holidays and, ultimately, leaving school for ever. In order to begin to meet this responsibility we must have some concept of a curriculum. Let us be sure we know what we mean by this. Any teacher

operates a curriculum. A curriculum is what is actually done in a classroom, what course is followed. To this extent a curriculum is *inevitable*. However, at this point there are disagreements and confusions that must be faced if we are to be clear about the nature of curriculum decisions and our own teaching. To begin with there is often a confusion between 'curriculum' and 'syllabus'. It might therefore be helpful to define a syllabus as a notated curriculum. We do not necessarily need to write out a curriculum but if we do specify something of the curriculum in written form then we have produced a syllabus. Although every teacher operates some kind of curriculum, it is more rare (in music) to lay one's hands on a syllabus and, strangely, when there is a syllabus people often say 'but I don't follow it'. In other words, it seems hard to make the syllabus properly describe the objectives and activities of the curriculum. For this reason many teachers abandon the idea of declaring or notating their curriculum and some would even say that they prefer the flexibility of *not* following any laid-down course. It is indeed very easy to criticise curriculum documents on the grounds that they make teaching rigid, that they do not allow for the unexpected, that they ignore the individual responses of pupils, that they go out of date quickly and that they do not really get to grips with the 'deep structure' of the subject but tend to trivialise it. It is indeed true that while general curriculum statements tend to be vague and platitudinous, a specific syllabus does often appear to be misconceived or trivial.

All this may be true but what is the alternative? Is it really the case that most music teaching in our secondary schools is well done when there is no declared curriculum or syllabus? We doubt it. The lack of clear and principled thinking in curriculum documents is probably symptomatic of an inadequate grip on music education issues. The abandoning of any attempt to make curriculum statements most often stems from inability, not from high principles of 'flexibility' and 'integrity'. There are, however, a few very able teachers who would argue that they proceed experimentally on the basis of providing rich experiences with unpredictable outcomes. Yet if we observe them at work we notice that they do initiate activities in particular ways, often highly structured, that they do seem to know what is important as against what is peripheral and that they have some pretty clear idea as to what counts as good, or acceptable, or inadequate work. In other words, they have a clear conception of what is involved in music and the ways in which students can be organised to get going musically. They have evolved strategies through experience and they can usually be articulate about them when asked.

Most teachers, by definition, are *not* exceptional and welcome some form of specific curriculum statement. It is indeed more honest and useful to have a publicly declared curriculum than a hidden one. If it is public it can be challenged and changed, shared with others and developed. Preparing a curriculum document is a spur to the thinking and professional practice of any teacher but there is no need for everyone to, so to speak, invent the wheel. New and insecure teachers especially would be helped by some existing framework, for not only are they learning to cope with children and trying to understand their subject but they are expected to be curriculum developers, innovators and evaluators. This is asking rather a lot and it is surely reasonable that some guidance be given, especially to people who are entering the profession or changing jobs; that there is some professional sharing.

Who then is to formulate the curriculum? In Britain this is not considered to be the responsibility of the HMIs, nor is it the mandate of the music advisers. Head teachers have responsibility for the curriculum of their schools but this is usually delegated to heads of departments. In Music the head of department may be the only music teacher in the school or may in any case say to colleagues 'feel free to develop your own ideas'. Lecturers in colleges and universities might want to make curriculum suggestions but there is no certainty that these will be acted upon or even considered in the schools. All this seems very wasteful. It is surely possible to formulate a framework for a secondary school music curriculum that can be shared and that is well-founded in clear thinking and good practice. The day-to-day decisions about method and material must be left to each individual teacher exercising judgement about particular circumstances, but the principles that underpin what is done and the rationale for the curriculum can and ought to be agreed.

The previous chapters of this book demonstrate a way of generating curriculum activities that stays close to music through composition, audition and performance, where we are always looking for structure and expressive character. What we have to attempt now is the development of a structure for this kind of work. It may help to organise the issues if we address ourselves to four questions, all of which need to be answered if we are to describe a curriculum in terms that will convince other people and help the practitioner.

1   Why is music on the school timetable?
2   What is to be learned?
3   Which activities and materials are appropriate?
4   How shall we organise our resources?

1   WHY IS MUSIC ON THE SCHOOL TIMETABLE?

A colleague in school once told us that at a parents evening he was accosted by the father of a pupil at school and asked two questions. What is the value of music? and Why is music in the school curriculum? In the four minutes allowed for conversation with each parent he had to formulate convincing answers. It is not uncommon for pupils too to want to know why music is in the curriculum. The first answer is the quick and immediate one. It runs something like this. Consider any cohesive community, what we call a culture. We shall not find music absent. Sometimes it will be linked with ceremony, ritual, dance, story telling and even magic and sometimes it will be separated into such specifically musical things as symphonies, pop songs or Indian ragas. There is certainly no need to defend the role of music. It is highly valued in any culture. The more difficult question is the second. Why is music in school? After all, it might be argued that there is plenty of music happening in the wider community and that school is an inappropriate place for musical activities. Here the justification hinges on the quality of what is actually done in the school. There can be no case for music done badly and where it is, every reason for weeding it out of the timetable. On the other hand there is every justification for supporting music when it is done well and when the school *extends* beyond what can be casually acquired outside; unless we believe that the role of schools should be limited to certain basic activities such as reading, writing, arithmetic and elementary science. If this is the case then the school day could be radically shortened and the school leaving age lowered. If schools are to be regarded as basing their curricula on the important and significant activities in any culture, then music is an obvious candidate.

It is important to give answers to these questions for other people but it is even more important to tackle the issue of the nature and value of music and its place in the curriculum *for ourselves* on another level. We have to know as professionals what is valuable about music and what lies behind the curricu-

lum decisions. In order to get some clear idea of where we stand
on this we shall need to strip away some dead wood of tangled
philosophies that have cluttered our way over the last decade or
so. It will be necessary to be fairly cryptic in outlining these
positions, though we hope not unfairly so. There are indeed two
apparently conflicting views that have confounded much good
work and set teachers against one another, dividing instead of
uniting professional aspirations.

The first of these, and the oldest, is the perspective that sees
education primarily as the transmission of some kind of *cultural heritage*. Accordingly, people undergoing education, and
especially children in school, are to be given information and
skills that will enable them to participate in the accepted main-
stream cultural setting. This in turn helps to perpetuate and
confirm the structure and content of the culture. This is *why*
we would have music on the timetable. The implications for
general music education are well-known. We would look for
familiarity with the master works, for an historical perspective
on music, for a knowledge about and, possibly, skill with
traditional 'instruments of the orchestra', for a degree of musical literacy, for concert-going habits, for a repertoire of community songs. In the case of the student learning to play an
instrument under specialist guidance, we would be initiating
him or her more rigorously into a long tradition of craftsman-
ship, probably through a well-developed system of instruction
assessed by carefully graded examinations.

Now all of these activities *can* have great value if they are
undertaken for better reasons than passing on the 'cultural
heritage', as though it were a kind of property or territory, and
if they are seen in a stronger educational perspective. As it
stands things often go wrong. Many students become alienated
from the master-works and appear to collide with the culture,
the territory, that the teacher represents, or, if they acquiesce,
may become knowledgeable *about* composers and their works
without commitment to real experience of them. Concert-going
habits are *not* generally established and the repertoire of 'community' songs are *not* those songs valued by the real community
outside of the school. For the instrumental player, sensitivity
is frequently obliged to go underground in deference to the
acquisition of skills and far too many students give up instrumental lessons than would be the case if there were something
intrinsically satisfying in the activity. The quest for any common 'cultural heritage' in multi-ethnic urban schools seems

doomed to failure from the beginning, and the most powerful musical experiences seem most frequently to occur outside of the constraints of formal education.

The second view, sometimes called 'progressive', is in sharp contradiction to the 'traditional' picture, so rudely caricatured above. The central article of faith here is that we begin with *the child as an unfolding personality* and not a mere recipient of a culture. Accordingly, the emphasis is on *learning* rather than teaching, on the development of the imagination, on discovery and above all, on *creativity*. Thus, instead of accepting and perpetuating the *status quo*, we look for development of the ability to influence and change the culture. In music education we would put an emphasis on composition or improvisation, on experimentation with new sound materials, on small-group or individual activities rather than large choirs or bands. We would look for involvement with contemporary music, defined alternatively as either the music of *avant garde* composers or pop music, though it is rare to find progressive teachers embracing both simultaneously. General music in schools is seen as very different from specialist instrumental tuition and the whole apparatus of examinations becomes suspect because it imposes an unwelcome uniformity and in any case, attempts to measure the unmeasurable — the personal development of differing individuals. This is *why* music is valued then: it helps people to develop as people.

Once again, the fundamental assumption gives rise to distortion of otherwise valuable activities. Teachers often abdicate from teaching altogether in the interests of children 'discovering' for themselves, or from a sensitivity to the creative processes of students. The music of the *avant garde* is not espoused by many and a good proportion of the students may feel that the school has no right to institutionalise popular music. The instrumental player goes his own way and shrugs off the low-level activity of the classroom, preferring to stay with the classical tradition, the rewards of examination passes and public acclaim. Worse still, most students seem not at all interested in the development of their personality through music. Out of school they find most satisfaction in talking, going to discos or, apparently, doing nothing in particular.

Let us attempt now to offer a less distorting fundamental, a pedal-note that underpins a tremendous possibility of progression and variation and at the same time gives us a sense of direction.

Our fundamental assumption is derived from noticing a relationship between the two extreme views already examined. It is essentially human to be at once an *inheritor*, part of a tradition, and an *innovator*, creatively striving within or against traditions. Each of us is, to a large extent, moulded by the culture in which we find ourselves but we also *shape* that culture through our individual actions. We are able to interact with the world in this way because we can manipulate such symbolic forms as language, maths, art and music. This symbol-making facility enables us to become aware of such things as personal history, the history of our culture, the thought, feelings and acts of other people, the movement of planets, the natural world around us; it also allows us to speculate, to predict and to make attempts to influence the future. Symbol-making is the supreme human gift. The psychological 'space' between one person and another, between an individual and his environment, is mapped out in symbolic forms. Music is one way in which people articulate their response to experience and share their observations and insights with others. It has something — though not everything — in common with the other arts, in that it is particularly well-adapted to illuminate those elements of human feeling which are fleeting and complex and the universal aspirations which most people share, whatever their culture.

Why we value music is ultimately not to do with belonging to a tradition or with self-development, as some have argued, but depends on a recognition that music is one of the great symbolic modes available to us. Initiation into this activity is what we look for. We might find ourselves drawn incidentally into a tradition or sub-culture, or may realise that we are developing as individuals: but these outcomes are by-products of doing music for its own sake, just as happiness is a by-product of something else, not a legitimate objective in itself.

No one has yet been able to explain in a totally satisfactory way how the arts function in a symbolic way, though many have tried. We shall not attempt to solve that enigma here but simply notice that artists of all kinds have taken extraordinary trouble to make sustained, complex and carefully articulated works and that people have responded to them as though they were significant, meaningful, symbolizing *something*. Something is communicated, something is transmitted, something is *known*. When a work of art stirs us it is more than simply sensory stimulation or some kind of emotional indulgence. Something important is happening, something illuminative, we are gaining in knowledge and expanding our experience. The same is true when we form music as composers or perform it: the act of shaping music is a purposeful attempt to articulate something meaningful. It need not be complex or profound, earth-shattering or of cosmic proportions but it will be expressive and structured and just as 'objective' as the spoken or written word, an equation or a map.

If we have taken rather a long time over the first question it is because it is the most important. If we have in our minds an inadequate answer we shall have very low voltage behind our everyday actions. If we give confused answers we shall deceive ourselves and mislead others.

2   WHAT IS TO BE LEARNED?

This question may seem at odds with our contention that discovery is central to musical activities. Can we say what is to be learned in advance? How can we predict what may be discovered? Of course we cannot predict every outcome of a particular event or project, that is what makes teaching a perpetual challenge. We can, however, have a good idea of some of the things that will need to be learned sooner or later. For example: in *Chapter Four* we discussed the idea of simple compositions in pairs using a repeated sound and a contrast. Although we could not predict exactly what the children might produce we do know that a principle will be learned if the compositions are to be effective. It is that too much repetition is boring and too many contrasts are confusing. This will be what is learned: that is to say, what is taken away from the music room and remembered when the actual composition is forgotten; what can be applied to other music, including that by 'professional' composers. This is what *learning* means. It is a change of skill, disposition or understanding that survives the immediate activity. In this particular case people may have differing views as to what counts as too much repetition, this is something capable of considerable refinement; but the principle will still hold. This is a very important point which is not always grasped. We have always to ask not only what the activities are but also what is being learned *through* them. Once we recognise that *learning* is involved in musical activities we can also see that sometimes the process needs to be sequential. For example: in *Chapter Three* we were concerned with rhythmic development and movement. Teachers sometimes make things difficult by not recognising that there is a hierarchy of skills and concepts involved in handling patterns of metric rhythm. The first thing to establish is *pulse*. Is it steady or unsteady? Can we hear and make differences between faster and slower pulses (tempo)? Can we make a pulse get gradually faster or slower? The next stage is the recognition and control of *accent*. Some pulse sounds are louder than others and this may give a feeling of heaviness or lilting or marching rhythm. The recognition and control of *metre* comes next. Is the pulse organised in two or three time? Finally we might expect control of rhythm patterns and imitation and invention of *ostinati* or answering phrases. So often this cannot be achieved because the control of steadiness and accent is poor and so things fall apart, the rhythm cannot hold!

In America and to a lesser extent in Australia, music curricula have been devised which specify sequential learning outcomes of this kind. Lists of what are called concepts are built up based on the four dimensions of sound we identified in *Chapter Four*, pitch, timbre, time and loudness. Sometimes these multiply into literally hundreds of terms which children may come to understand and which involve aural, manipulative and notational skills. These lists may include such items as phrase, unison, scale, tonic, vibrato, cadence, dissonance, glissando and modulation. (These were taken at random from one list of about 300 terms.) The trouble with this way of working is that we may start looking for material — songs, a recording, a particular activity — in order to develop one such concept. It then becomes very easy to violate the principle that delight in *music* is the aim. The song, the recording, the activity has to be good as *music* and should not be chosen just because it illustrates a particular rhythm pattern or because it exemplifies ternary form or because it develops control of pitched sounds. Of course we want such learning to take place and we also want to bring about a grasp of structure and a recognition of expressive character. (Recognition of ternary form by itself hardly counts as understanding structure, which is a question of relationship. How is the middle section different from the rest? Is there a strong contrast? Is anything the same?) With this in mind, such a curriculum does support the insecure teacher who needs to be helped to structure class activities to some obvious purpose. It also helps teachers of younger children, who may have no specialist musical education, to develop their own musical skills and awareness.

Music teachers and educationalists in the UK have resisted this sequential form of curriculum building, which emphasises planning and predictable outcomes, and in doing so have made life more difficult for all but the exceptional teacher. There may indeed be good reasons for not listing concepts of this kind. One of them is that they can only function as a check-list; they certainly could not be remembered. They also tend to clutter up the approach to music. For example, we may inci-dentally note that a tune is in two-four time but be more taken with its particular march-like qualities, its expressive character. Listening for the metre may actually impede listening to the music, in the same way that identifying the notes of a melody as they present themselves will destroy the feeling of line, shape and expressiveness. At the same time, there is much to be said for organising the music curriculum of primary schools in a planned, developmental sequence.

The problems for secondary schools is that pupils arrive with radically different levels of ability and experience and (let it be said) often with diminishing enthusiasm for general music courses in classes of thirty. The solution seems to be to organise the secondary curriculum in a *modular* rather than a completely sequential way. The advantage of a modular scheme is that there can be several new beginnings and this gives a certain freshness to music in secondary schools. This is why the mater-ial in this book is organised in modules rather than as a linear course. Each project can be started at a level relevant to the experience of the class, probably with a problem to be solved. There will be a culminating point, which may be a series of small-group performances, a whole class composition assembled from small-group contributions or a performance on record and tape of related items composed by children and 'professional' composers. In this way there will be a sense of *encounter* which is quite different from the steady progress at the heart of a sequential, pre-planned course. Yet in day-to-day teaching there must be awareness of possible learning outcomes and some kind of strategy to bring these about. We certainly look for bonuses but in addition to and not instead of a steady income. The following scheme will remind us of the areas in which learning can take place relating to the activities of com-position, performance and listening.

Learning Outcomes

Skills (knowing how)

(a)   *aural* — discriminating in pitch, time, loudness, timbre

(b)   *manipulative* — handling instruments, the voice
(c)   *notational* — using a range of notations

Information (knowing that)
(a)   *technical vocabulary*
(b)   *historical background and social context*

Understanding (knowing it)
(a)   *structure* — the relationship of part to part and part to whole based on forms of repetition and contrast
(b)   *expressive character* — mood, atmosphere, level of tension, gesture, feeling, emotion

Values (knowing what's what)
revealed through preferences and level of commitment

Music teaching often seems directed towards objectives in the area of Skills and Information. Yet, as we have tried to show in earlier chapters, musical Understanding is just as susceptible to the formulation of objectives and really is the crucial element in any general music curriculum. Values can probably be 'caught' but not taught. We are always looking for signs that pupils are coming to value music but we obviously cannot predict how and when this might happen. For these reasons we ought to concentrate on the area of Understanding, for it is obvious that Skills and Information will be musically empty without it and there will be no basis at all for the building of Values. It is probably true to say that what pass for value judgements among many of our young people are the result of social (peer group) conditioning rather than direct experience and real understanding. It is here that schools and teachers have a vital role.

While acknowledging that it is one of the main purposes of education to enhance and extend the range of what is valued, we also recognise that there can be no attempt to tackle value changes head-on in the classroom. Since we look for development here but cannot predict it, we can leave Values out of curriculum details while remembering that if music is not valued more because of our work we shall have been wasting our time.

At some stage we need to make judgements about the *level* of achievement we might expect in secondary schools. It is at this point that teachers themselves need to enter the curriculum debate and say clearly what levels of expectation they have in the first year, the second year and so on. It is impossible to specify this from the outside of any particular school with its special problems and opportunities.

3 WHICH ACTIVITIES AND MATERIALS ARE APPROPRIATE?

Here we need to consider the kind of people our pupils are. When they enter secondary school they are towards the end of what may be described as a 'skill-hungry' age. If there is to be any systematic attempt to develop skills in general music classes in secondary school then this is the time. The first year could be rich in opportunities. The manipulative skills of handling instruments and voices; aural skills of identifying and discriminating pitch, time, loudness levels and timbre, notational skills ranging from simple sight-singing to following, using and making graphic scores: there is plenty to be doing! What Bruner describes as a 'desire for competence' (cf Chapter One) is very strong at this time among normal children. Related to this is the spirit of curiosity and the exploration and development of sounds, bringing them into meaningful relationships and making compositions in small groups, whole classes and perhaps as individuals. The kind of activities indicated in Chapters Three, Four and Five would be appropriate.

The emphasis higher up the school must be towards those other 'natural energies', 'aspiration to emulate a model, and a deep-sensed commitment to the web of social reciprocity'. As children mature into mid-adolescence these become increasingly important motivating forces. Accordingly, the emphasis in general classes may not be so much on acquiring skills but on the social context of music and the puzzle that radically different groups of preferences present. The phenomenon of pop music, music from different cultures, contemporary music; these will move more sharply into focus as we attempt to understand something of the social and cultural framework within which music is located. Whether we are concerned with skills or the informational background, the fundamental musical activities of composition, performance and listening must still predominate. Otherwise we shall be teaching something else, not music.

It may be helpful to consider an example drawn from Chapter Three where the activities are related to conventional rhythms. A class is to pick up the song *Five Hundred Miles* from a teacher's performance in an easy flowing style. The tempo is to have an 'easy swing' and there may be a light accompaniment. The children are to 'finger-click' the pulse with alternate hands. The accentuation is to be felt and pointed by using different sounds (clapping, tapping, knee-slapping) to express the strong/weak alternation. The rhythm pattern ♫ ♫ is then used in an *ostinato* fashion along with other simple patterns, especially ♩♫ The processional *Wedding at Troldhaugen* (by Grieg) and the stamping, exuberant *Padstow Song* can also be performed, heavy, robust, strong (cf Chapter Three for other possibilities.) In all of these the simple pattern ♩♫ is obvious but each time different in expressive character which is determined by speed, loudness, strength of accent and smooth or detached vocal lines. These seem appropriate activities for many classes of twelve year olds. Small groups may compose using the simple rhythms but choosing speed, loudness and relative smoothness to communicate a particular expressive quality. The composition should be interesting, that is to say, should have some structure, perhaps a contrast at some stage and a return to the ideas of the beginning. It ought not to be long.

It would be possible to vaguely occupy a class without really getting them going in any of these musical ways or to get them going but not be aware of the *learning* possibilities. In Chapter One we distinguished between activities and learning outcomes. It may help us here to indicate *some* of the outcomes we might be looking for during these activities with rhythmic elements. They can be formulated as objectives, each item prefaced by the phrase — *the pupils should be able to* —.

UNDERSTANDING (structure and character of music)	SKILLS (aural, manipulative notational)	INFORMATION (technical vocabulary, historical and social context)
Perform *Five Hundred Miles* in an easy, flowing style.	Control 'body' percussion sounds as an accompaniment.	
	Identify the rhythms: by sight and sound.	Define pulse, accent, rhythm pattern, accompaniment.
	Notate these rhythms.	
Identify and make music that is heavy, smooth, strong, stamping, processional.	Demonstrate ensemble skills across a range of speeds and loudness levels.	Say: which country Grieg came from; what happened at Padstow; what the words of *Five Hundred Miles* are about
Employ repetition and contrast to make interesting pieces.		
Notice that in the 7th bar of the song the tune has moved away from the starting note from then 'wants' to return.	Identify the sound of the 'home note' and 'away' notes at the end of phrases.	

(In the Appendix the reader will find a purpose-designed two-year curriculum framework along these lines. It might be interesting to compare the levels of expectation here with those in British schools.)

It would be possible, though very cumbersome, to 'notate' any lesson or project using this model and for some teachers it may be helpful to try as a way of analysing and extending what is involved in any activity. This would be useful in the case of student-teachers or where an activity is being tried for the first time. For normal practice though it is probably easier to answer a series of questions along these lines.

i   What activity is relevant for the particular group and manageable, given the resources?
ii   What elements of musical understanding are involved?
iii   What skills will have to be developed?
iv   What information is relevant and helpful?
v   How is the enterprise to be organised?

After the event(s) we might ask:
vi   How much was achieved?
vii   Which elements can be taken further?
viii   Are there signs that the activities are coming to be valued?

After a few sessions we might ask:
ix   Are we extending the range of music that is being experienced?

In an even simpler form the questions reduce to two:
i   Is there any sense of achievement for the pupils?
ii   How much direct musical experience is there?

4   HOW SHALL WE ORGANISE OUR RESOURCES?

Here we are not thinking merely of hardware and space but, more importantly, of time and teachers. It may be that after one year of intensive general teaching we should look at an alternative way of using *all* our teachers, including the instrumental teachers. Without increasing our teaching forces it would be possible in many secondary schools to re-organise classes into purpose groups. What stands in our way are the traditions that have grown up over time.

In Britain we inherit two traditions of music education, especially in secondary schools. The first of these derives from the private school system and essentially sees the music educator as 'director of music' who runs the band, choir and orchestra, who manages the chapel choir and organises individual instrumental teaching. The second tradition stems from the state school concept of the class lesson where music is treated like any other 'subject' with allocated slots of large-class time for general music education. In most secondary schools today the two systems run side by side, with instrumental teaching managed on a rota basis (controversially) withdrawing students from other classes to work with visiting specialist teachers. The regular music teacher thus wears both hats, that of director of music and class teacher, coping with classes all day, and rehearsals, performances and instrumental administration in spare moments and after school. The strain is enormous but difficult to avoid. Teachers feel that the classes are the real reason for their employment and yet the choirs and orchestras are necessary, not only to put the music department on the map of the school in the eyes of staff and parents but also to give opportunities to the minority of students who have a special interest in and ability with music.

We ought to think hard about this for several reasons. In the first place, class music has suffered from a 'bad press', mainly because of poorly formulated objectives based on an inadequate rationale, but also because a standard class of about thirty students once or twice each week may not be the best setting for music. Larger or smaller groups formulated on some kind of selective basis will be necessary for different activities within the areas of composition, audition and performance.

Secondly the one-to-one instrumental lesson is not only economic nonsense but is also educationally unsound. Children and adults learn a great deal from each other through imitation and emulation. Careful listening and watching are essentially basic requirements for the advancement of instrumental techniques and a *group* rather than an individual with a teacher is a much better setting for the encouragement of these essentials. Not only this, but the individual lesson will often stop short of performance and be confined to skill acquisition. A group on the other hand can be an *ensemble* where the presence of actual music can be felt from time to time and responsiveness to pieces can be developed along with technical accomplishment. Nor need we confine ourselves to performance. A group of, say, ten students can be an improvising ensemble on occasion, that is to say, functioning as composers. Members of such a group can also play the role of auditors to each other in performance. Group teaching is an area well worth attention in the future.

In case this is thought to be impracticable, let us take a specific instance. Two classes are timetabled for music at the same time and two instrumental teachers are available along with the two class teachers. This raises the possibility of four groups, perhaps of different sizes. One group might be working — composing and/or performing with classroom instruments, another might be a guitar and recorder group, another might be a wind ensemble, the fourth could be listening to and discussing records. Spaces for these activities will have to be found but this is not impossible at a time when the number of children at school is falling. The listening group might alternate with the classroom instrument group while the others remain as they are for the second and third year of the secondary course.

We should make it clear here that these instrumental groups are not primarily there just for the development of instrumental skills but for a broad musical education. There ought to be a record player in the room; there should be discussion as well as performance; there will be some improvisation. The aspiring player will be identified and helped towards the local music centre, a private teacher or to some extra-curricular arrangement in school but every member of the group should benefit, not just the minority.

The reasons behind such groups is obvious. Remember Bruner: a desire for competence; wanting to emulate a model, commitment to social reciprocity. The instrumental group is a 'grown up' activity imposing its own disciplines and involving the growth of competence. The most effective models are those of the peer-groups as we can observe when adolescents imitate pop idols. The social interaction in such a group can be very stimulating to the teacher as well as the group members.

All this requires a new breed of teachers, especially instrumental teachers, who are able to organise material for group involvement, to think through the implications for composition, performance and listening and the learning outcomes involved. In other words the instrumental teacher has to be able to do what the class teacher is expected to do. It could be that the most useful person in a music department will be the class teacher who plays an instrument or the instrumental teacher who is willing to undertake in-service education.

If the first year of secondary school is to be an explosion of structured and purposeful activities and the second and third years are to be organised in the way described here, then the fourth and fifth years can be built on what has gone before and, possibly, might aim towards the new, and we hope radically improved 16+ examination. One thing is certain: once purpose groups are established in earlier years we will be reluctant to let them go towards the end of a school career when they seem to have more relevance than ever to the world outside of school. The 'purpose' here will have become the purpose of the students. The teachers' purposes will be working themselves out. Music, which is so obviously valued in the world will be valued in the school.

Appendix

In August 1981, Keith Swanwick and a colleague, Charles Plummeridge, were asked to visit Singapore to advise the Government on a music curriculum in four selective secondary schools. Their brief included a survey of physical facilities, recommendations on conversions and sound insulation, field trials of selection procedures, suggestions on resources and materials, consultations with teachers and Ministry officials, visits to schools and the specification of a four year music curriculum designed to culminate in a 16+ examination (at the time the Cambridge 'O' level). All this was carried out and documented in a Report during the nine days of the visit, except for the last two years of the curriculum framework which were dependent to some extent on changes in the 16+ examination.

The bare framework of the first two years' curriculum is included here since it might be of interest to see how a curriculum can be formulated along the lines indicated in this book. The reader should bear in mind that this proposal was submitted as a basis for discussion with teachers and has since changed as a result of this. It is also a response to a *very specific* educational context. Singapore operates a selective system of schooling. That is their affair and we make no comment on the principles behind such a policy. The teaching style is somewhat 'formal' and is closely geared to examination success. The music course happens to have been conceived for those children in the top 50 per cent range according to general academic ability. These factors caused us to propose a framework that may appear rather 'traditional' to some music teachers in the UK. However, to others, and certainly to colleagues in Singapore, the proposals may appear to be wider and more 'experimental' than present professional practice. The content could be different in several ways but we believe that the approach is sound.

ELECTIVE MUSIC COURSE:
CURRICULUM OUTLINE FOR YEARS ONE AND TWO

Objectives

Note: In order to clarify the objectives in this scheme, the reader should bear in mind that each item should be prefaced by the phrase — The pupils should be able to . . .

UNDERSTANDING (Structure and Character of Music)	SKILLS (Aural, Manipulative, Notational)	INFORMATION (Technical Vocabulary; Historical and Social Background)	RELATED MATERIALS
Identify and make different phrase shapes in sound. eg eg	Notate phrase shapes (a) Graphically eg (b) In staff notation using first five notes of the major scales of C, G and F	Identify phrase signs. Name relevant scales Use appropriate vocabulary — forte, piano, crescendo, diminuendo, phrase, etc. Recognise signs:	Simple folk, national and popular songs. *Approach to Music* *Oxford School Music Books* *Something To Sing*
Recognise contrasting and repeated phrases in a melody.	Identify the number of phrases in a short melody.	Use the terms 'binary' and 'ternary' for particular phrase structures.	
Recognise and describe the expressive character of different pulse speeds.	Identify and clap or tap 2, 3 and 4 metres at different speeds using pulse values only. Control slow and fast pulses in clapping. (ie keeping steady)	Say what is meant by pulse, accent, bar, time signature.	
Compose short pieces choosing speed, levels of loudness and known rhythm patterns (unpitched)	Read rhythm patterns such as:	Identify crotchet, quaver, minim, dotted minim.	eg Beethoven, *7th Symphony* (Slow Movement) Grieg, *Wedding Day at Troldhaugen*
Recognise the expressive character of contrasting sections in specific pieces.	Identify longer binary and ternary forms aurally and from notated music.	Compile a list of composers and names of pieces. Give some limited biographical details.	eg Grieg, *Norwegian Dances* Keyboard music of Bach, Handel, Purcell, Bartok, Schumann, Schubert, Beethoven. Songs from many countries.

UNDERSTANDING (Structure and Character of Music)	SKILLS (Aural, Manipulative, Notational)	INFORMATION (Technical Vocabulary; Historical and Social Background)	RELATED MATERIALS
Identify expressive qualities of contrasting timbres, eg 'Shrill woodwind, Sombre brass, 'warm string' tone. 'aggressive' percussion.	Discriminate between various instrumental groups played on records.	Name families of orchestral instruments and other general groupings eg Wind band, String orchestra, Swing band. Chinese orchestra	eg Messiaen, *Et expecto resurrectionem mortuorem;* Gerhard, *Concerto for Orchestra.* Elgar, *Serenade for Strings.* Barber, *Adagio for Strings.* Britten, *Young Person's Guide to the Orchestra.*
Use classroom and orchestral instruments (and piano) to compose and perform pieces based on instrumental groupings.	Control instruments Demonstrate ensemble and conducting skills. Use graphic and conventional notations/for compositions and performances.	Write the names of relevant composers. Use terms like avant garde, ethnic music, timbre, texture.	eg Penderecki, *Trenody for the Victims of Hiroshima,* Balinese Gamelan Music, Recordings of Chinese Orchestras. Salaman, *W. Class in Concert.* Picken and Port, *Ancient Chinese Tunes**
Give sensitive performances of contemporary music written for the classroom.	Work in a disciplined manner in large ensembles. Display more refined control of instruments.	Interpret 'new' notational symbols such as:	Self, *New Sounds in Class* Dennis, *Experimental Music in Schools* Pieces by such composers as Rands, Bedford, Dennis, Paynter.
Identify expressive character of major versus modal melodies. Recognise 'stabilising' effects of single and double drones and melodic ostinati.	Sight sing, play and write from dictation using all the notes of the major scales of C, G, D, F, B♭. Recognise Aeolian mode beginning on A, E and D.	Use the concept of 'sounds together' (Beginnings of harmony) Name relevant composers and define terms such as drones and ostinati.	Handel, *Pastoral Symphony* from *Messiah.* Brahms, *Serenade in D,* 1st Movement. Tchaikovsky — *Arabian Dance* from *Nutcracker Suite* Indian Ragas Folk songs from many countries

UNDERSTANDING (Structure and Character of Music)	SKILLS (Aural, Manipulative, Notational)	INFORMATION (Technical Vocabulary; Historical and Social Background)	RELATED MATERIALS
Recognise 'completeness or incompleteness' in music in relation to harmonic content.	Identify the point of change in two-chord songs. Distinguish chord I from V in the context of a harmonised tune.	Use terms like triad, harmony, perfect and imperfect cadence. Employ the chords I and V	Any songs requiring two chords for their harmonisation. eg *Clementine Down in the Valley Turn the Glasses Over.* Oxford School Music Books Basic Goals in Music
Compose harmonies for given melodies in major keys. Describe the expressive effects of different figurations.	Play three-note chords (I and V) on instruments. Handle simple arpeggio figurations of these chords.	Define terms such as alberti bass and arpeggio.	Thackray, *Creative Music in Education* Yorke Trotter, *Principles of Musicianship*
Perform simple pieces while others follow the score. Listen for and discuss structure, expressive character, particular instrumental effects.	Identify individual instruments in an ensemble context. Follow a score with limited instrumentation, starting with piano scores, trios, quartets, etc.	Name instruments. Give technical details and historical background. Use terms, eg reed, embouchure, mouthpiece valves, keys, etc. Name relevant composers. Interpret technical signs and terms used in the scores.	Fiske, *Score Reading, Bk 1* Bach, *Anna Magdalena Book* Bartok, *Mikrokosmos* Port, *The Lantern Song Book* Bartok, *Concerto for Orchestra*
Identify more extended structures, perceiving elements of contrast and repetition, eg Theme and variations, Rondo. Perceive effect of contrasted short movements through listening, performing and composing.	Demonstrate longer spans of attention and memory and increasing control of compositional and technical devices.	Identify forms, composers and terms such as episode, decoration, development, subject, coda, introduction.	Handel, *Harmonious Blacksmith* Dohnanyi, *Variations on a Nursery Theme* Mozart, *Horn Concertos* Mozart, *Eine Kleine Nachtmusik.*

UNDERSTANDING (Structure and Character of Music)	SKILLS (Aural, Manipulative, Notational)	INFORMATION (Technical Vocabulary; Historical and Social Background)	RELATED MATERIALS
Recognise the effect of quicker notes on character of music. Identify military, lilting and other effects created by dotted notes.	Recognise and read such patterns as [musical notation examples in 2/4, 3/4 and 4/4 time] Recognise and use appropriate rests.	Use the terms semiquaver, semibreve, dotted note, etc.	*Oxford School Music Books.* (Senior Preliminary, I, II and III) Handel, *For Unto us a boy is born* (*Messiah*)
Compose well-structured pieces using newly introduced rhythm patterns. Perform rhythm canons.	Demonstrate further grasp of rhythmic patterns in longer phrases. Hold on independent part (rhythm only).	Use terms such as imitation, round and canon giving examples.	*Approach to Music* Books 1 and 2 Folk songs
Compose short pieces using major and minor as forms of contrast. Perform melodies in major and minor keys.	Differentiate between heard major and minor melodies major and minor triads. Write tunes from dictation using mainly step movements in relative minor to known major keys.	Write out minor scales. Use the term harmonic minor and describe the scale structure. Explain the term relative minor. Define 'accidental'.	Strauss, *Also Sprach Zarathustra* Schubert, *Trout Quintet*, Theme and Variations. Elgar, *Enigma Variations* (Theme Variation III, Nimrod) Paynter and Aston, *Sound and Silence*

Note: This outline was eventually slightly modified as a result of meetings with the teachers concerned. In particular, a number of Chinese songs were incorporated at our request. What we have here is, therefore, a 'local' curriculum, though the principles are generally helpful, whatever the local context.

Bibliography

ABRAHAM, G (editor) *The Concise Oxford History of Music*, Oxford University Press, 1979

ABRAHAM, G (general editor) *The History of Music in Sound*, Vol 1 Ancient and Oriental Music, OUP, 1957

ASCH, M (editor) *124 Folk Songs*, Robbins Music Corporation, 1965

AUDEN, W H (editor) *et al An Elizabethan Song Book*, Faber, London, 1957

BENNETT, R *Enjoying Music*, Books 1 and 2, Longman, London, 1978

BROADWOOD, L & FULLER MAITLAND, J *English County Songs*, J.B. Cramer & Co Ltd, (undated)

BRUNER, J *Towards a Theory of Instruction*, Harvard University Press, 1966

BURNETT, M (editor) *Music Education Review*, Vol 1 Chappell, London, 1977

CAMPBELL, I *Come Listen*, Ginn & Co, London, 1969

DOBBS, J, FISKE, R & LANE, M *Ears and Eyes*, Teachers Book 2, OUP, 1980

DWYER, T *Teaching Music Appreciation*, OUP, 1967

FAWCETT, B *Exploring Composers*, Harrap, London, 1980

FLOYD, L *Indian Music*, OUP, 1980

JAQUES-DALCROZE, E *Rhythm, Music and Education,* Dalcroze Society, 1921

LABAN, R *Modern Educational Dance*, Macdonald & Evans, 1948

LANG, P *Music in Western Civilisation*, W.W. Norton, New York, 1941

LEACH, R & PALMER, R *Folk Music in School*, Canbridge University Press, 1978

LEWIN, O *Dandy Shandy*, *12 Jamaican Folk-Songs for Children*, OUP, 1975

LLOYD, A L *Folk Song in England*, Paladin, 1975

PAYNTER, J *Hear and Now*, Universal, London, 1972

PAYNTER, J & ASTON, P *Sound and Silence*, CUP, 1970

RENOUF, D & SMITH, E *Approach to Music*, OUP, 1968

SACHS, C *Rhythm and Tempo*, Dent, 1953

SADIE, S (editor) *The New Grove Dictionary of Music and Musicians*, Macmillan, 1980

SCHOLES, P *Music: The Child and the Masterpiece*, OUP, 1935

SELF, G *New Sounds in Class*, Galliard, London, 1967

SORRELL, N & NARAYAN, R *Indian Music in Performance*, Manchester University Press, 1980

SWANWICK, K *A Basis for Music Education*, NFER — Nelson, Windsor, London, 1979

TAYLOR, D *Music Now*, Open University Press, Milton Keynes, 1979

TILLMAN, J *Exploring Sound*, Galliard, London, 1976

VULLIAMY, G & LEE, E *Pop, Rock and Ethnic Music in School*, CUP, 1981

WALKE, O *Folk Songs of Trinidad and Tobago*, Boosey & Hawkes, London, 1970

Music index